Critical Thinking Skills for Education Students

Second edition

STUDY SKILLS IN
EDUCATION

Critical Thinking Skills for Education Students

Second edition

Lesley-Jane Eales-Reynolds,
Brenda Judge,
Patrick Jones and
Elaine McCreery

Learning Matters
An imprint of SAGE Publications Ltd
1 Oliver's Yard
55 City Road
London EC1Y 1SP

SAGE Publications Inc.
2455 Teller Road
Thousand Oaks, California 91320

SAGE Publications India Pvt Ltd
B 1/I 1 Mohan Cooperative Industrial Area
Mathura Road
New Delhi 110 044

SAGE Publications Asia-Pacific Pte Ltd
3 Church Street
#10-04 Samsung Hub
Singapore 049483

Editor: Amy Thornton
Development editor: Geoff Barker
Production controller: Chris Marke
Project management: Swales & Willis Ltd,
Exeter, Devon
Marketing manager: Catherine Slinn
Cover design: Wendy Scott
Typeset by: Swales & Willis Ltd, Exeter, Devon
Printed in Great Britain by CPI (UK) Ltd, Croydon

Library of Congress Control Number:
2013936981

British Library Cataloguing in Publication Data

A catalogue record for this book is available
from the British Library

ISBN 978 1 44626 840 7
ISBN 978 1 44626 841 4 (pbk)

Contents

The authors

Prior to joining Kingston as Pro Vice Chancellor (Education), Professor **Lesley-Jane Eales-Reynolds** was the Director of Learning, Teaching and Pedagogic Research at the University of Westminster. She received her BSc in microbiology from the University of Wales and her PhD in immunology from the University of Bath. After post-doctoral work at the Max Planck Institute and St Mary's Hospital, London, she joined the University of Surrey.

A professor of immunology and health science education since 2003, she has led innovations in teaching in the health-related sciences. A recipient of a National Teaching Fellowship (NTF) in 2001, she became one of the first senior fellows of the Higher Education Academy in 2007 and PFHEA in 2012. She is a founding member and past chair of the Association of National Teaching Fellows and a past board member of the Higher Education Academy.

She is currently leading an international project (funded by the NTF scheme) looking at the use of Web 2.0 tools to develop critical thinking skills through the development of authentic assessment artifacts.

Brenda Judge is a senior lecturer at Manchester Metropolitan University, where she teaches on both the undergraduate programme ITT and the postgraduate programme. Previously at Edge Hill University, she taught on undergraduate and postgraduate programmes and educational studies. While at Edge Hill she led year one of the undergraduate programme. Brenda trained as a primary teacher and has taught in primary schools and also been a head teacher of two different schools. Her main teaching area is English and Teaching Studies, and she has particular interest in how to manage children's learning and the development of reading. Her Master's degree focused on Primary School Management, in particular the appraisal of head teachers. Brenda's first book *Learning to Teach in the Primary Classroom* was published in 1995 and a further book on education issues has followed since then. She is currently working with colleagues on a new book on the English curriculum post-2012.

Patrick Jones trained as a primary teacher and became a head teacher before taking up his post at Manchester Metropolitan University. His first publication was in 2008 and focused on his passion for music. He has written a number of musical scores, which have been performed by recognised amateur orchestras. Patrick is now retired, and as well as volunteering in some Cheshire schools as a musician/teacher, he is studying a degree in Fine Art.

Elaine McCreery is Head of Primary, Early Years and Education Studies programmes at Manchester Metropolitan University. While at Roehampton University she taught on primary education programmes. She led the MA Education programme and a Return to Teaching programme for teachers who had taken a career break. Elaine trained as a primary teacher and has taught in both primary and secondary schools. Her main teaching area is Religious Education and she has particular interest in children's spiritual development, teacher identities and the work of faith schools. Her Master's degree focused on Religious Education and Primary School Management. In her PhD work, she explored how primary teachers contribute to the spiritual development of children. Elaine's first book *Collective Worship in the Primary School* was published in 1993, followed by other books and articles on RE and Teacher Education. She is currently working on developing initial teacher education programmes to meet the challenges and expectations of primary education for future generations of teachers.

Acknowledgements

Every effort has been made to trace the copyright holders and to obtain their permission for the use of copyright material. The publisher and author will gladly receive any information enabling them to rectify any error or omission in subsequent editions.

1. Critical thinking: why is it important and what is it anyway?

Introduction

In this chapter we will explore what we mean by critical thinking. You will begin to understand that critical thinking is essentially a questioning, challenging approach to knowledge and perceived wisdom. You will understand that critical thinking involves examining ideas and information from an objective position and questioning this information while being aware of the influence of your own values, attitudes, experiences, emotions and personal philosophy.

Learning outcomes

Having worked through this chapter you should have an understanding of:

- why critical thinking is important;

- the essence of critical thinking;

- the process of critical thinking;

- how your own values, experiences, emotions and attitudes impact upon your critical thinking.

Why is critical thinking important?

Employers have identified critical thinking, critical analysis and problem solving as key skills that they are seeking in graduates, but rarely find. These abilities underpin good management and leadership. Critical thinking skills will be essential to your study and your professional practice, giving you the ability to think both critically and objectively about an issue and present a well-constructed argument. Developing critical thinking skills will also equip you with some of the attributes required in entrepreneurs and in those who are able to take a sustainable approach to living and working.

So what is critical thinking?

From a very early age, we learn to question. Parents always seem to dread their small child asking them 'why?' because it is often an endless litany. However, this questioning is vital to help us make sense of our world and in developing our ability to think critically.

When we talk about critical thinking, we are not using the word 'critical' in a negative way. For example, the statement *I don't like the jacket that she's wearing* is being critical about someone's fashion choices. However, it does not involve critical thinking. In fact, this simple statement is an example of something that must be avoided in critical thinking (i.e. biasing our judgements because of personal preferences).

Critical thinking requires us to question everything, including things that may normally be accepted *de facto,* such as the statement *the world is round*. How do you know this is true? By taking a challenging approach to knowledge and perceived wisdom, you develop your own understanding and enhance your personal knowledge of the world.

It must be remembered that critical thinking means different things to different people and it will depend on your ontological and epistemological leanings. (Ontology is the science relating to the nature of being; epistemology is the aspect of philosophy that deals with the theories relating to the sources, nature and limits of knowledge.) However, at its very basic level, critical thinking is about taking a questioning approach to everything.

To be a good critical thinker you will need to be:

* willing to question your own views and those of others (just because something is in print or on the web, it does not mean it is true);

* open-minded to the ideas and views of others;

* able to make (positive and negative) judgements;

* able to discriminate between sources of evidence and recognise their authority and authenticity;

- self-confident enough to explore and question the evidence/literature and its implications;

- able to recognise the strengths and weaknesses of your own thought processes and argument development;

- honest in facing your own biases/prejudices;

- flexible in considering alternatives and opinions;

- willing to reconsider and revise views where honest reflection suggests that change is warranted;

- able to re-present your thinking and argument in an improved form.

The process of critical thinking

A great deal of what is taught in universities is theory rather than 'fact'. Although based on evidence that may appear to be factual, most information results from the critical thinking and interpretation that writers and researchers have drawn from their analyses of relevant data. They propose ideas to explain what is going on in the world and gather research evidence to support or refute these ideas. Actually, academic debate is founded on an exchange of ideas or theories. If one person puts forward an idea or theory, then other people will often put forward alternatives. When you, as a student writer/researcher, enter a debate, you become part of this ongoing argumentation, contributing to the body of knowledge surrounding the issue through using your critical thinking skills.

One of the most important aspects of critical thinking is personal knowledge creation. This we do by:

- identifying our existing knowledge and experiences in relation to a particular issue;

- considering our stance in relation to that issue (a reflective process which involves our emotions and values);

- collecting authoritative evidence, which may contradict or support our stance;

- critically analysing (studying its meaning, structure and validity) and evaluating (making a judgement about) that evidence;

- using it to develop our own knowledge and understanding.

This process may potentially alter our own viewpoint. Thus, critical thinking involves interpretation, analysis, evaluation, inference, explanation and metacognition (the awareness or analysis of one's own learning or thinking processes) (Facione, 1998). These processes allow us to put forward a meaningful argument to persuade others to our point of view and thus to contribute to the collective knowledge base.

Before we explore these elements of critical thinking in a little more depth, I should insert a note of caution. There are many interpretations of the meaning of the term 'critical thinking' and many proposals as to the skills and attributes required to be a good critical thinker. These vary by discipline, distinguishing what is thinking and what is implementation of thinking or practice and country of origin. You will find that the language used in different disciplines to explain the same phenomenon will often differ. This has led to a lack of consensus across disciplines as to exactly what constitutes critical thinking and what skills students need to demonstrate in order to be good critical thinkers. However, a critical evaluation of precisely what is meant by this language can lead to the identification of a core set of skills and attributes that are the same at a fundamental level regardless of discipline.

In the references and further reading section of this chapter you will find other articles, books and websites that give a range of descriptions of critical thinking skills and how they vary within disciplines. We have chosen Facione's framework since it covers the fundamental skills which have been identified by a range of authors, as well as informing one of the most widely used standardised tests of critical thinking skills – the California Critical Thinking Skills Test.

Interpretation

When we read something, our understanding of what we read is dependent upon our own experiences and existing knowledge. Think of a small boy learning to read the sentence:

John has a ball.

If the boy has never seen a ball, he will not understand the meaning of the sentence. Similarly, imagine you meet a woman and you ask her what she does, and she replies:

I'm an immunologist.

You may have some understanding of what immunology is, but not necessarily what an immunologist actually does. However, if you work in a clinical laboratory, you are likely to have worked with an immunologist and so will have some understanding of what the role entails.

If you have no understanding of something you hear or read, then you cannot critically analyse it or evaluate its worth in relation to your existing knowledge or that of your wider community. Thus, the first step in interpretation is understanding. Having understood something it is necessary to be able to express its meaning or significance, i.e. your interpretation of what you have read, and this will be coloured by your prior knowledge, values and personal experiences (including emotions). So, for example, you read an article in the newspaper about global warming – is it real or not? The article seems to put forward some persuasive arguments against its existence. However, you have been to Greenland and seen the glaciers melting at an unprecedented rate – are you likely to believe the article or seek to find fault with its logic and argumentation because your personal experience suggests it is wrong?

Practical task

Find an article in a newspaper and read it initially to see if you understand what it is about in general. Then see if you can identify the data upon which the writer has drawn to create his/her interpretation. Explore your own interpretation and what it is that the writer is trying to persuade you to believe. Do you agree with his/her interpretation? If not, why not?

When you have done this exercise, reflect on what it has taught you, or what it has enabled you to develop further through practice.

Analysis

In order to be able to think critically about a particular subject, it is necessary to carry out a detailed examination of the elements that comprise it, in order to facilitate understanding or discussion of the subject. This examination allows you to try to find meaning in the information or data, and this is the process of analysis.

How many times have you heard people say: *Just give me the facts*. However, facts are only someone else's interpretation of the information/data, and they will be coloured by the individual's own agenda. A good example of this is in advertising where, in order to persuade you to buy its product, a company will quote the proportion of people interviewed who thought the product actually did make them younger, or slimmer or fitter. We'll talk more about persuasion and opinion in a later chapter.

Reflective task

What is wrong with the following statement?

> *76 per cent of people asked thought taking X for 6 weeks made them more intelligent.*

You need to analyse exactly what this statement is telling you. What other information would you want before you might consider investing in, or using, the product?

The process of analysis should enable you to identify both the actual relationship between statements and the intended relationship – these may not always be the same thing. For example:

- Statement 1. An independent survey was undertaken to canvass the opinion of people about the closure of the car park.

- Statement 2. The decision to close the car park was approved by a majority.

- Conclusion. The closure of the car park was the result of an unbiased majority opinion.

These statements are intended to imply that the closure of the car park was democratically agreed in an unbiased way, i.e. *the closure of the car park was the result of an unbiased majority opinion.* However, what does it really tell you? The survey was independent – but independent of whom or what? What does it mean by 'independent'? This can be open to a range of interpretations in this context. Who were the people who were canvassed? Also, *the decision to close the car park was approved by a majority.* Who were these people – the same ones that were canvassed or those attending a meeting about the closure of the car park? How were they chosen to take part? How many of them were there? Thus the actual relationship between these statements is not as clear as might be assumed. The survey may have been truly independent (unbiased) but it does not say that the survey demonstrated that the majority of people canvassed approved the decision. Although this is a rather superficial example, it does demonstrate the need for you to question everything constantly. Do not assume that because something comes from an authoritative source it is beyond criticism.

Evaluation

When you have understood what you have read and analysed exactly what it is telling you, then you need to evaluate whether or not the evidence or argumentation used to persuade you to a particular point of view is valid or not.

Evaluation is the process during which you make a decision about the contribution an existing source of knowledge can make to your argument or discussion. For example, when researching a particular issue or subject, you may discover information that is contradictory to your own understanding or to that provided by other sources. Do you abandon your argument in favour of the contradictory one or do you 'stick to your guns'? If the latter, how are you going to persuade others to your point of view?

Imagine that you are required to write an essay on a topic that necessitates exploring the existing literature on the subject. Having undertaken a search on the web or in the library, you have identified a number of resources that appear to have relevance to the topic. Some of these contradict each other. How will you determine which resources you will use and cite in your essay? The following provides some guidance in this respect.

Where was the material published?

Papers published in journals are usually (although not exclusively) peer-reviewed – this means they have already been judged to be acceptable by professionals in the field. Material published through government agencies and professional body websites are also usually thought to be authoritative. However, just because it is published, do not fail to question it – experts can get it wrong too!

Who has published the material?

If a resource is not from a journal or authoritative source (as described above), it does not necessarily mean that it should be excluded. The authority of the author is also important. Leading experts in their field may publish opinion pieces on their personal websites or blogs. However, beware, because many individuals (lacking what we might consider to be appropriate credentials) also publish their own views and opinions on websites and blogs. It is a matter of looking at what they are saying and exploring whether or not their conclusions are based upon appropriate evidence or premises (propositions upon which an argument is based, or from which a conclusion is drawn). Remember, opinion pieces are just that – the encapsulation of someone's opinions which may be coloured by their experiences, emotions or values. They may try to persuade through rhetoric (the art or study of using language effectively and persuasively), rather than through reasoned argumentation.

Are the conclusions valid?

The resources you have identified will all have a 'message' or conclusion about the subject in question. The authors will have arrived at this conclusion by constructing a persuasive argument based on evidence or premises. You should be able to determine if a conclusion is valid, i.e. if the evidence presented supports the conclusion drawn and also if the argument used to produce the conclusion is based on sound, rather than unsound, premises or rhetoric. This ability to deconstruct arguments and to identify their elements is absolutely key to the process of analysis and therefore critical thinking. We will explore this further in the next chapter.

Inference

Inference is the part of the critical thinking process where we start to consolidate our own knowledge with that which we have found, in order to create new understanding. With this knowledge we can propose new interpretations of existing ideas or even new ones, and draw conclusions for our arguments that are valid and reasonable. This is typically shown in books that are written about unsolved mysteries such as the identity of Jack the Ripper. The 'facts' of the case are relatively well documented – who the victims were, how they died and where. The authors have then looked for other evidence and information and have drawn inferences that suggest the Ripper may have been the Duke of Clarence or Walter Sickert (the artist), among others. The prevailing opinion is going to be influenced by the author or authors who produce the most persuasive argument backed up by reliable evidence.

Explanation

Absolutely key to being a good critical thinker is the ability to explain your reasoning clearly and coherently, i.e. you must be adept at making your thinking plain and comprehensible to your audience. It is more than just providing a descriptive narrative (which is important to set the scene) and must offer reasons for the decisions or choices you have made in the process of arriving at your conclusions. This is all part of the skill of argumentation, which will be described in Chapter 2.

Metacognition

One of the challenges of critical thinking is the requirement to be self-aware, and to understand how our own experiences and biases may influence any conclusion we may draw from data we read and how we communicate them or translate them into practice. For example, a newspaper story tells of how an animal rescue team found a dog in very poor condition and arrested the owner and charged him with cruelty. As a dog lover, you may be keen to see that owner severely punished. However, what the article may not tell you is that the case was never brought to court because the owner had very recently taken the dog from a rescue centre and was actually trying to help it recover.

It is really important to be aware of how your own perceptions and prejudices can influence your argument and therefore make it vulnerable to discredit. For example, a study that sets out to determine from the literature the impact of teaching critical thinking skills to students but ignores any paper or report that is purely qualitative is as flawed as one that does not look at the quality of the research design in the papers considered. Thus, really understanding your own perceptions and being able to interpret and analyse your responses and reactions to situations are very important aspects of critical thinking. In practice-based professions, in particular, this process of self-reflection is well developed and will be explored in Chapter 7, when we explore developing our critical thinking skills through analysing our own writing.

Summary of key points

I think we can see from this first chapter that critical thinking requires a range of attributes and abilities/skills, all of which can be developed. In the literature there is no one agreed definition of critical thinking or the skills it involves. For the purpose of this book, we have chosen to look at the work of Facione and Facione (2007), which is based on qualitative research and which incorporates many of the skills and attributes identified by others. The skill of self-reflection is recognised as a key element of critical thinking in some disciplines. In Facione's framework, metacognition is the recognised skill that incorporates reflection.

It is important to remember that critical thinking is not a linear activity: there may be iterative cycles of interpretation, analysis, evaluation, inference, explanation and metacognition with extensive feedback loops. Each cycle helps to inform and hone the argument that we are developing to persuade others to our point of view. We have talked a little about the process of argumentation in this chapter. In Chapter 2, we will look at it in greater depth.

References and further reading

Facione, PA (1998) *Critical Thinking: What it is and why it counts*. Millbrae, CA: California Academic Press.

Facione, PA and Facione, NC (2007) Talking critical thinking. *Change: The Magazine of Higher Learning*, 39(2): 38–45.

Facione, PA, Facione, NC and Giancarlo, C (2000) The disposition toward critical thinking: its character, measurement, and relationship to critical thinking skills. *Journal of Informal Logic*, 20: 61–84.

Krathwohl, DR (2002) A revision of Bloom's taxonomy: an overview. *Theory into Practice*, 41: 212–218. Available online at: **www.unco.edu/cetl/sir/ stating_outcome/documents/Krathwohl.pdf** (accessed 4 February 2013).

Martin, DW (2006) An 'infusion' approach to critical thinking: Moore on the critical thinking debate. *Higher Education Research and Development*, 25: 179–193.

Moon, J (2008) *Critical Thinking: An exploration of theory and practice.* New York: Routledge.

Websites

www.merriam-webster.com/dictionary/metacognition: free online dictionary.

www.thefreedictionary.com: free online dictionary.

2. Developing a critical mindset: deconstructing argument

Introduction

In the previous chapter we looked at the skills required to be a good critical thinker. At the simplest level it involves taking a questioning approach to everything. If you are asked to form an opinion on something, then you need to question the existing evidence. This will usually be presented as some form of argumentation, e.g. 'based on X and Y, then Z is true'. In order to arrive at your own viewpoint you need to be able to analyse the arguments with which you are presented and determine whether or not they are valid. We shall look at this process in this chapter.

Learning outcomes

Having worked through this chapter you should have an understanding of:

- how basic and complex arguments are constructed;

- the way in which valid conclusions can be identified from premises;

- the role of subjectivity, objectivity, ambiguity and rhetoric in argumentation;

- how being able to deconstruct arguments helps to develop your critical thinking skills.

What do we mean by argument?

When using the word 'argument' in relation to critical thinking, we are not talking about a disagreement but a means of persuading others to your point of view. An argument usually consists of one or more premises (statements of fact on which the argument is based) and a conclusion. For example:

- Premise 1: The sign by the road works has fallen over.

- Premise 2: There is a very strong wind blowing.

- Conclusion: The wind has blown over the sign.

Obviously, there may be other reasons why the sign has fallen over, such as it was hit by a car, or someone maliciously knocked it over – I'm sure you can think of others. However, without that knowledge, then the conclusion given is quite logical, but may not be the only explanation.

Practical task

Find a news report or editorial on the web or in a magazine or newspaper.

Identify the focus of the report and try to identify one of the writer's conclusions. Then try to identify the premises upon which that conclusion is based.

It is important to be able to identify conclusions that authors have drawn and the premises or data upon which they have based these conclusions. You need to exercise your judgement – are the conclusions logical and supported by the evidence or are they based on false premises? A false premise is a statement that does not support the conclusion drawn. Using the example from above:

- Premise 1: The sign by the road works has fallen over.

- Premise 2: There is a very strong wind blowing.

- Conclusion: The sign is broken.

Premise 1 still supports the conclusion that the sign may indeed be broken because it has fallen over. However, premise 2 is a false premise because it does not support our conclusion. A better premise would be:

- Premise 2: The sign was hit by a car.

Notice that in the above argument, the premises are statements – which may be factual, but they depend on the arguer's perception/recollection of what he/she experienced. This does not make them invalid, but you should be aware of this.

Reflective task

Following on from the exercise above, would you judge that the author had drawn logical conclusions from the stated premises? If not, how would you rephrase them?

Premises are the statements that must support the point of view you are trying to communicate, i.e. your conclusion. When constructing your argument, it may be more effective to develop subconclusions based on relevant premises and to use those to support your overarching conclusion. These are known as nested arguments, where the conclusion from one becomes a premise for the next part of the argument. So, for example:

- Premise 1: The school has invested a lot of resources into devising a highly nutritious menu for school meals.

- Premise 2: Students who don't have school meals tend to have an unbalanced diet.

- Conclusion: It is better for all students to have school meals from a nutritional perspective.

Now we use the conclusion from this argument as the first premise for the following part of the argument:

- Premise 1: It is better for all students to have school meals from a nutritional perspective.

- Premise 2: Our current resources do not allow us to cater for all students.

- Conclusion: We need to invest in our catering resources.

Practical task

Find another editorial or news report and examine it to see if nested arguments are used. Give the examples you find and make a judgement as to whether or not you feel the premises truly support the conclusions drawn.

Subjectivity, objectivity and ambiguity in argumentation

Subjectivity

It is important when analysing an argument to avoid being persuaded to a point of view because the author has used rhetoric or subjective constructions. ('Subjective' means based on or influenced by personal feelings, tastes or opinions.)

It is essential that you are able to justify your position by providing evidence about the subject in such a way that your judgements and conclusions are seen as objective, and not based on false assumptions or premises biased by your own values, attitudes, experience, emotions and personal philosophy.

You need to be particularly discriminatory about:

- statements of 'fact' where the author suggests that the point is obvious and needs no further discussion (i.e. 'It is perfectly obvious that . . .; It is an accepted fact that . . .');

- unsubstantiated comments or statements and anecdotal evidence;

- unbalanced arguments or those based on false premises or assumptions;

- bias (whether political, personal or professional);

- the credibility of sources of information used to substantiate claims and arguments.

Practical task

During a seminar James stated that 'some parents, especially those from deprived backgrounds, have little understanding of the needs of their children and are unable to make appropriate judgements'. Megan asked him on what evidence he was basing this statement. James realised that what he had said was very subjective.

Try to reword James's statement to make it less subjective. When you have finished, compare the two and make a list of the words you removed or changed to make the statement less subjective. What type of words were these?

Objectivity

At the heart of critical thinking (and, indeed, critical reading and writing) is the notion of 'objectivity' (the opposite of subjectivity). Being objective means that you read, write and think without bias. You take into account all the facts and possible explanations and draw on available evidence, questioning its authenticity and the logic of the underlying argument used to persuade a reader of the expressed point of view. It is important to distinguish where an author is putting forward a reasoned argument based on evidence rather than offering an explanation for something which might be based on the writer's own personal beliefs and therefore potentially biased. Expressing personal opinions is subjective. However, the opinions can become more objective if you subject them to rigorous questioning.

Objectivity means standing back and weighing the evidence, even if you disagree with something. You can remain objective by examining the positive and negative aspects of all issues, evaluating a selection of different theories on issues and using the third person instead of the first person. However, as a great deal of your writing will involve reflecting upon and analysing your own practice (particularly if you are a trainee teacher or educational practitioner), you will write predominantly in the first person (e.g. *I believe that this reflects the true opinion of the majority*, or *In my opinion the argument given is biased and based on false assumptions*), which may make it more difficult to appear completely objective. One way to achieve this is to write in the third person (e.g. *The data shown reflects the true opinion of the majority*, or *The evidence suggests that the argument given is biased and based on false assumptions*).

Practical task

Select a copy of a professional journal or newspaper (which may be online) and read the editorial or readers' comments section. Try to identify the words that make the section emotive and/or opinionated (subjective), perhaps by highlighting or underlining these words. Now read a straightforward (news) article from the same journal or newspaper. Compose your own list of the differences in the language and presentation. Is one more objective than the other? If so, why do you think that is?

Ambiguity

Two common problems can lead to confusion when thinking critically about a subject. We've already talked about subjectivity, and now we need to consider ambiguity. A word is ambiguous if it has several different meanings. For example, 'school' might specifically refer to a building where children are taught or a management structure within a university – or even a collection of fish! Therefore, unless the word is used within a context that makes it clear which meaning is intended, it is sometimes difficult to distinguish between them.

For example, the statement *The school was really big* might really excite a fisherman but would not necessarily please parents who were concerned that in a large school their child may not receive enough attention. By changing the sentence to: *The school was really big – it had 15,000 pupils,* we have immediately shown the context for the statement.

Reflective task

How might you make the context even clearer given the potential interpretations for the word 'school'?

The above demonstrates the importance of contextualisng any words you use that might potentially be misleading because they are ambiguous.

Even once all ambiguity is removed from a term, people may still disagree about its meaning because of their past experiences. Allowing your own views, values and biases to colour your interpretation of a statement or set of evidence (i.e. being subjective in your analysis) can still lead to problems.

For example, take the problem of interpreting the concept of partnership in the context of students and their universities. Many institutions now have a student charter or partnership agreement and recognise 'students as partners', but what does that mean? Two people may agree precisely about what that partnership is (e.g. they may accept that it is an agreement between the university and students), but may disagree about the role of each party and the range of activities to which it relates. This may be influenced by personal philosophy, values and beliefs. For example, academics may see it as their role to encourage students to learn for themselves, whereas students may see it as the role of the academic to tell them everything they need to know to get their degree. This shows that even when a concept is agreed by all parties, there are differences in the way the different parties interpret the meaning and application of the agreement owing to its subjective nature.

Rhetoric

Rhetoric may be used as an instrument to manipulate listeners or readers and persuade them to a particular point of view without providing tangible evidence. For example:

- Premise 1: Recent scientific evidence has demonstrated that global warming is threatening our very future.

- Premise 2: 'Fat cat' businessmen are ignoring the issue of sustainability as long as they can line their pockets.

- Conclusion: We are destroying our world and leaving a lethal, toxic legacy for our children and their children.

You may strongly believe that global warming is real and is threatening our future, but as a critical thinker you should not be persuaded by the first premise, asking:

- What recent scientific evidence?

- Is there evidence to the contrary?

- How valid are these studies?

I'm sure you can think of other questions. The second premise is purely based on rhetoric, raising images in our minds of the economic crisis and bankers' bonuses.

- Where is the evidence that businessmen are ignoring sustainability?

- Are all businessmen acting that way?

The conclusion drawn is based on rhetoric. If we were to accept premises 1 and 2 as true, then the conclusion may be valid but the way it is phrased is designed to pull on your heart strings. Who among us wants to think of our children and grandchildren suffering because of our own actions?

The example demonstrates how, without providing specific evidence, but using emotive language, it is possible to persuade individuals to your viewpoint. Some of the greatest orators in history have persuaded people to their views because of their ability to elicit emotional reactions from their audience. This does not mean that their arguments are necessarily false, but it does mean that one has to be very aware of one's own reactions to particular approaches to persuasion.

Some examples of rhetoric or subjective vocabulary, phrases, clauses and statements are:

- emotive language (e.g. shaven-headed thug, work-shy, troublemaker);

- stereotypes and generalisations (e.g. tea-drinking English, famine-ravaged Africa, the youth of today, the elderly, the disabled);

- persuading words and phrases (e.g. surely, obviously, as everyone knows).

Practical task

Look for an article on the web, possibly from a blog, which is trying to persuade you to a particular viewpoint. Try analysing the argument and see if you can identify whether or not the author is using rhetoric – and if the writer's premises and conclusion(s) are valid.

Taking a questioning approach

It is important to remember that to be a good critical thinker you should always examine everything with a questioning approach. Just because something appears to be accepted wisdom, it does not mean there is not an alternative explanation. For example, Piaget and Donaldson's views differ on how children develop. Piaget argued that children's thinking does not develop entirely smoothly. Instead, there are certain points at which it 'takes off' and moves into completely new areas and capabilities. Piaget saw these transitions as taking place at about 18 months, 7 years and 11 or 12 years. This has been taken to mean that before these ages children are not capable (no matter how bright) of understanding concepts and/or ideas in certain ways. Piaget's proposal has been used as the basis for scheduling the school curriculum.

On the other hand, Donaldson's theory (argument) focuses on the concept of embedded and disembedded thinking. Thinking that is embedded or placed in a familiar context makes 'human' sense and is more easily understood by children who are able to reason with it. When children are asked to do something that is unfamiliar or unrealistic their thinking is disembedded and it fails to make sense.

Donaldson challenged Piaget's theory of children having a ceiling on their thinking. She encouraged practitioners to seek out what children are able to do rather than focusing on the things they cannot do. She believed that in order to educate young children effectively, practitioners must try to present things from a child's point of view.

What this means for you is that, while there is often a dominant prevailing viewpoint on a particular issue, there will be alternative viewpoints that you can explore and analyse through literature and experience (both your own and that of others). You can always find alternative viewpoints if you look hard enough.

Practical task

Look on the web for information about an issue that has recently been in the news. Try to seek out two opposing views and then analyse the argumentation in the articles. Try to identify their conclusions, subconclusions and the premises upon which they base the argument. Are the interpretations different because of personal bias and an inability to look at the evidence objectively or are the conclusions based on false premises? Which side do you take and why? Examine your own reasons for your choice – are they biased by your values, experiences or personal beliefs?

The exercise you have just undertaken demonstrates that critical thinking is the ability to examine thought processes and argumentation – both your own and those of others. To be able to do this effectively, it is necessary to be willing to question your own views and be open-minded to the ideas and views of others. You also need to be confident enough to recognise that just because something is in print or on the web (in the public domain) does not mean it is true.

Be aware that you need to cultivate a healthy scepticism of:

*   statements which begin with *It is obvious that*;

*   arguments which are unsubstantiated and unbalanced, or which have a particular political, professional or anecdotal bias (as opposed to researched evidence).

Summary of key points

In Chapter 1, we explored the type of skills/attributes you need to develop to be a good critical thinker, including the need to be able to understand and demonstrate argumentation. In the current chapter we have looked at how you can decipher arguments on the basis of whether or not they are founded upon objective and valid premises.

As a good critical thinker, it is necessary for you to exercise discrimination and to judge which information sources are authoritative and use them to enhance your own knowledge and understanding of a particular subject. This skill is also required to help you judge whether the arguments of others are based on valid, reliable information. In recent years, this skill has become known as information literacy. This term encompasses more than just discrimination and judgement: it includes the ability to source reliable information and to manage the material you find/use. Previously, information literacy has not been explicitly associated with critical thinking, but many of the skills used by someone who is information-literate are those of a good critical thinker. We will explore information literacy in the next chapter and highlight the similarities and differences between the skills required for this and for critical thinking.

References and further reading

Cottrell, S (2011) *Critical Thinking Skills*. Basingstoke: Palgrave MacMillan.

Donaldson, M (1984) *Children's Minds*. London: Fontana.

Lapakko, D (2009) *Argumentation: Critical Thinking in Action*, 2nd edn. Bloomington, IN: iUniverse.

Norgaard, R (1997) *Ideas in Action: A guide to critical thinking and writing*. New York: Longman Press.

Piaget, J (1972) *The Child's Conception of the World*. Towota, NJ: Littlefield Adams.

Websites

http://io9.com/5888322/critical-thinking-explained-in-six-kid+friendly-animations (accessed 7 January 2013): This is a site with short, easy-to-understand videos that explain logic, argumentation and critical thinking. Good for students of any age.

http://oxforddictionaries.com/definition/english/subjective: free online dictionary.

3. Information (digital) literacy

Introduction

The advent of the twenty-first century has seen a massive explosion in the rate at which knowledge is created. This is largely due to the rapid growth of the internet, greater connectivity speeds and wider accessibility. Everyone has the opportunity to 'have their say' and to present themselves as experts in any particular field. This repository of 'knowledge' is designed to give us access to information, which through careful thought and reflection may help us make greater sense of our world.

Learning outcomes

Having worked through this chapter you should have an understanding of:

- the meaning of digital literacy and how it relates to critical thinking;

- how to manage information and resources relevant to your work.

Information literacy: definitions and relation to critical thinking

The Chartered Institute of Library and Information Professionals defined information literacy as *knowing when and why you need information, where to find it, and how to evaluate, use and communicate it in an ethical manner* (**www.cilip.org.uk/get-involved/advocacy/information-literacy/Pages/ definition.aspx**).

In addition, the Joint Information Systems Committee defines i-skills as *the ability to identify, assess, retrieve, evaluate, adapt, organize and communicate information within an iterative context of review and reflection* (**www.jisc.ac. uk/uploaded_documents/JISC-SISS-Investing-v1-09.pdf**).

However, perhaps the most inclusive definition is that from the Research Information Network, which accepts both of the definitions above and states:

> *It is important to adopt a broader interpretation of information literacy, which (i) recognises that 'information' must be taken to include research data; and (ii) clearly also encompasses the ability to manage, and where appropriate preserve and curate one's own information and data.*
> **(http://www.rin.ac.uk/our-work/researcher-development-and-skills/information-handling-training-researchers/information-lit)**

Table 3.1 demonstrates that information literacy skills map those identified by Facione (2005) as essential to critical thinking, with the addition of 'searching', 'managing' and 'organising' information. We would argue that, in this digital age, these skills are essential to enable us to practise and develop the other skills associated with critical thinking. If you cannot find relevant information in the first place, then evaluating its validity and reliability is impossible.

So, having identified these additional skills, let's explore what we mean by them and how we might develop them in practice.

Searching for information

One of the key roles of a library or learning resource centre is to provide the expertise to help you learn how to search for information in an effective and efficient manner. In a recent study, we have shown that students still tend to access books and journals to support their learning (Clarke et al., 2013) and so it is still important for you to learn how to use library cataloguing systems. However, with many journals and books now being made available electronically, it is also important to know how to access information via the web.

Web searching

Although not many students will admit it, many start searching for resources using an online search engine such as Google, Safari, Chrome, Internet Explorer or Opera. These are able to search the web and the relevance of the information they return is dependent on the search terms used. These may be words or groups of words that define what it is you are looking for.

Skill	Critical thinking skills (Facione)	Information literacy (CILIP)	Information literacy (JISC)	Information literacy (RIN)
Interpretation	✓	✓ (How to use information)	✓ (Adapt)	✓
Analysis	✓	✓ (Knowing when and why you need it)	✓ (Assess)	✓
Evaluation	✓	✓	✓	✓
Inference	✓			✓ (Implicit because it relates to one's own data)
Explanation	✓	✓ (How to communicate it)	✓ (Communicate)	✓
Metacognition	✓	✓	✓ (Iterative context of review and reflection)	✓
Searching		✓ (Where to find information)	✓ (Identify)	✓
Managing			✓ (Retrieve)	✓ (Specifically one's own data)
Organising			✓	✓ (Preserve and curate one's own data)

Table 3.1 **Comparison of skills required for critical thinking and information literacy**

CILIP, Chartered Institute of Library and Information Professionals; JISC, Joint Information Systems Committee; RIN, Research Information Network.

Practical task

You are required to write an essay providing a critical analysis of our current research knowledge of the epidemiology of AIDS.

Think of the search terms or keywords you might use to source information on this and use them to carry out a search on Google.

How many hits did you get and what is your opinion of the relevance of the top ten hits?

Now try the same search but using Google Scholar. What has happened to the number of hits and the relevance and quality of the results?

Try some other keywords and see the difference between the two sets of results you get.

The exercise above should show you how you can improve the outcomes of your searching by using a more appropriate search engine.

Many disciplinary fields have their own databases, the content of which may or may not be searchable by engines such as Google or Google Scholar. They tend to include only materials from recognised publication sources (i.e. peer-reviewed research journals; educational publishers) and thus provide you with a good starting point for evaluation of the quality and relevance of the publications. However, you must remember that even experts can make mistakes and just because something is published, you cannot take it at face value.

Your library should have a catalogue of the electronic resources to which you have access. These will include a range of databases as well as e-journals and books. Most databases work in the same way as search engines; they use the keywords you enter to search their resources. If you refine your keywords or key phrases, your search will be more focused to your particular research question. Since you may not complete your searching at one sitting (particularly for larger pieces of work such as dissertations), it is really important to keep a record of when and where you have searched, the search terms (keywords) you used and the number of hits returned. For example, imagine you are interested in the FIFA World Cup. If you were to undertake a search on the web between World Cup championships, you would get a very different set of hits to that which you would get during the World Cup. Indeed, during such a competition, the top hits on the web will change daily.

Managing and organising information

Recording the details of your searching is all part of managing and organising the information you are obtaining. Once you have completed a search, you will have a list of publications that you will want to explore further. Firstly, you will want to judge their relevance to your research question or topic of study. Then you will need to evaluate the validity of the methods used to gather any data, the interpretation of that data and the conclusions drawn. Finally, you will identify the new, relevant information that you will synthesise with your existing knowledge to help develop your own interpretation and conclusions about your research question. The problem is, you might find several relevant articles, all of which you need to evaluate before you draw your final conclusions. Some of those articles may be contradictory and you will have to develop your reasoning as to which point of view you are accepting. This means that you may need to revisit some of the articles more than once whilst developing your argument. In order to do this effectively, you need to organise and manage the information you discover. For some this may be as simple as keeping a record either on individual cards or in an Excel database. However, there are numerous computer programs that enable you to do this and much more. Examples of these are Endnote and Reference Manager and your library may be able to supply you with one of these. Alternatively there are free versions that you can download from the web, such as Zotero. All these programs have features in common. They allow you to record the important information from resources, including title, authors, publication data (e.g. journal, volume, pages, year), keywords and URL (if it's an online resource).

They also have the option to include the abstract of the article with these details and to append a copy of the article (if available) to the entry in the database. Perhaps the most important function of these tools is that when you do a search, you can automatically download this information into the citation manager – you don't have to type it in yourself. You can also add notes, so as you review the resource you can make notes of the important features in relation to your question as well as record the search terms you used, what search engine you used and when you accessed the information. This is really important because, like everything else, the web changes and what may be there today won't necessarily be so tomorrow. The joy of these programs is that the majority link to Word so that when you are writing your assessment, you can automatically insert references and compile your bibliography. Your library or learning resource centre may be able to offer you training in the use of the more popular reference managers. Many of them now also come with applications for use on mobile communication devices and allow collaborative use, facilitating group work.

Practical task

Find a reference manager, try a web search and load your results into your software. Then try adding notes about your search. As with all new programs the basics are intuitive but you need to explore to find the full functionality.

Once you get used to using a reference manager, you will be able to insert citations from your database automatically into your documents using appropriate word processors. The database will manage your bibliography so that if you later edit your work and delete a reference to a particular source, your reference manager will automatically remove it from your bibliography at the end of your work.

Practical task

Try inserting some references in a block of text in Word – they don't need to be accurate for the purposes of this exercise. Check the bibliography and then go and delete one or two and check your bibliography again to see if they have disappeared.

Plagiarism and copyright

We've just been discussing how to manage and organise the information you find. This is really important, so you don't end up duplicating effort because you know you read something somewhere, but didn't keep the details and so have to search again. It is also important for another reason. If you use verbatim quotes or figures from articles you find (on the web or elsewhere) it is really important that you attribute them, i.e. that you indicate whose original words or work it was. If you do not, it may be considered that you are trying to pass it off as your own and you will not only be in breach of copyright, but also you will be committing plagiarism. This is considered to be academic misconduct and you will be penalised (the penalties will vary from one institution to another but can be very serious). Students are often faced with the dilemma of how to paraphrase something that is considered to be accepted wisdom. The simple answer is that you do not have to do so. If something is so iconic, then quote and attribute it. This is perfectly acceptable practice.

Practical task

Below is a paragraph from a report looking at whether training or educational interventions have any impact on practice. Try to rewrite it so that you are keeping the most important points but so that the work is yours and not plagiarised.

A review of studies which looked at the effectiveness of printed educational material on changing provider behaviour concluded that it had only a small impact on practice (Freemantle et al. 1996). These studies all emphasise the need for an interactive educational experience which is appropriately contextualised if one is to bring about a change in practice. Indeed, an overview of systematic reviews of interventions to change provider behaviour concluded that multifaceted interventions were more likely to be successful (Grimshaw et al., 2001).

Freemantle, N., Harvey, EL., Wolf, F., Grimshaw, JM., Grilli, R., & Bero, LA. (1996) Printed educational materials to improve the behaviour of health care professionals and patient outcome (Cochrane Review). In: The Cochrane Library, Issue 3, Oxford: Update Software.

Grimshaw, J. M., Shirran, L., Thomas, R., Mowatt, G., Fraser, C., Bero, L., et al. (2001). Changing Provider Behavior: An Overview of Systematic Reviews of Interventions. Medical Care, 39(8), II-2-II-45

It is really important to appreciate that, just by changing the order of words in a sentence, you are not avoiding the charge of plagiarism. As a critical thinker, you should be able to absorb the message an author is giving and synthesise your own interpretation in the light of your own existing knowledge of the subject and your experience. If you really can't use your own words, then make sure you repeat the author's words verbatim, enclose them in quotation marks and add the appropriate citation.

It is also important to remember that, just because you can download something from the web, it doesn't mean that you can reproduce it in your own work. At the very least you must attribute it (the author of the resource, the date you downloaded or accessed it and the site from which you obtained it) but you must also check that its use is not restricted by copyright. This information should be available from the site. Many sites will have an acceptable usage policy which should include what use may be made of information and resources on the site.

Summary of key points

In order to develop your skills as a good critical thinker it is important to practise them. This can be done in a number of ways but getting practice at sourcing information and deciding whether it is reliable and valid is extremely important. The mass of information available means that it is also highly important that you know how to manage and organise it, as well as use it in an ethical way that does not lead to plagiarism. These are key elements of information literacy.

One definition of information literacy also includes the management and organisation of your own data, or that of others. Since arguments/ conclusions often are based on such 'evidence', it is important that you are able to analyse this data and interpret it either to allow you to make valid conclusions (if the data is your own) or determine if the author's conclusions are valid. This is what we shall look at in the next chapter.

References and further reading

Clarke, C, Eales-Reynolds, L-J, Gillham, D and Grech, C (2013) Online resource identification and use: are there disciplinary differences across students in higher education? ALT-J (Submitted)

Facione, PA (1998) *Critical Thinking: What it is and why it counts.* Millbrae, CA: California Academic Press.

Websites

www.apa.org/about/offices/directorates/pubs.aspx (accessed 18 December 2012): The American Psychological Association gives detailed information about all its electronic databases.

www.cilip.org.uk/get-involved/advocacy/information-literacy/Pages/ definition.aspx (accessed 18 February 2013).

www.eric.ed.gov (accessed 18 December 2012): Education Resources Information Centre (ERIC) is an electronic database of educational research and information, sponsored by the Institute of Education Sciences, USA.

www.informationliteracy.org.uk (accessed 18 December 2012).

www.jisc.ac.uk/uploaded_documents/JISC-SISS-Investing-v1-09.pdf (accessed 18 December 2012).

4. Analysing data and interpreting findings

Introduction

We all undertake research every day, whether it is to find the cheapest deal on a new television or finding the best resources to support an argument in your coursework. Many of the critical thinking skills we have been exploring are vital when you are engaged in research. At some point in your career, you will need to undertake research in relation to your professional practice. This may involve collection of new data or analysing that collected by others in order to inform a decision or to help you develop a persuasive argument for change. In this chapter you will explore the collection of data, the subsequent analysis of that data and how it informs your professional practice.

Learning outcomes

Having worked through this chapter you should be better able to understand:

- the different types of data with which you might work;

- how you might collect such data in a reliable and reproducible way;

- how to interpret and use the data you collect.

Different types of data and its analysis

There are fundamentally two distinctive types of data which can be collected, collated and analysed. These are quantitative data and qualitative data.

Quantitative data

The essence of quantitative data is that it is measurable on a numerical scale. This might be height, weight, length, depth, number, speed, etc. Research techniques that provide data resulting from measurement on a specified scale and numbers (or proportions) that need to be summarised, described and analysed are considered to be quantitative. The characteristics of quantitative data may be demonstrated and explored by drawing graphs and charts and by looking at population-based statistics such as means, medians, standard deviations and ranges. Further analysis allows the identification of patterns and relationships between data sets by comparing means, exploring correlations and performing other statistical tests such as multiple regressions or analyses of variance. Advanced modelling techniques may eventually be used to support sophisticated explanations of how the data informs our conclusions in relation to the original question. Our conclusions convey our interpretation of the data in relation to the original question or problem considered.

In order to understand the limitations of the conclusions one can draw from quantitative data, let us consider an example.

Worked example

A new fertiliser is supposed to make beans grow much faster and produce larger crops than an existing fertiliser. Your research question might therefore be:

> *Does the new fertiliser improve the growth rate and yield of beans compared to a standard fertiliser?*

In order to investigate this, you plant two lots of beans and give one the new product (A) and one the old (B). By measuring the growth rate (height versus time planted) and weighing the crop at a given time point (yield), you can compare the effects of the different fertilisers.

However, it is essential that all other factors (known as variables) that may affect growth rate and yield (such as the amount of light and water provided and the ambient temperature) are the same for both samples.

In quantitative methodology, you always assume that there will be no difference between the two (i.e. you assume a null hypothesis in this case):

There is no difference between the two fertilisers tested on the growth rate and yield of beans.

Having measured the two test samples, you calculate the mean growth rate and yield for each sample and compare these using a statistical test (in this case the student's t-test would be appropriate). You then look up your t-value in a table of probabilities that determine the likelihood that the result you have obtained is purely by chance. For example, if your t-statistic gives you a result of 95 per cent probability you can have considerable confidence that your null hypothesis is true, i.e. there is no difference between the two fertilisers. However if your result gives you only a 5 per cent probability that your null hypothesis is correct, then you can have considerable confidence that it is in fact wrong and there is a real difference between the two fertilisers.

This is how statistical analysis works – it increases your confidence in saying that there is a difference. However, it does not prove there is a difference and your confidence only relates to those two fertilisers with those particular beans in the exact environmental circumstances that occurred in your experiment. Since scientists can control variables in an experiment they sometimes forget that statistical significance still has its limitations and that the outcomes only relate to the exact experimental circumstances. Obviously in education, controlling variables that might impact on student learning is even more difficult and, whilst quantitative approaches are used, they are restricted to certain types of study.

Some basic analyses can be carried out using Excel, whilst more sophisticated analysis is likely to involve the use of a computer program such as SPSS. Your librarians should be able to help you with information about such packages and what is available in your institution.

Parametric versus non-parametric analyses

Quantitative data is usually based upon a particular population. The expectation is that, in relation to a particular measurement, the results will be 'normally distributed' i.e. for a set of data ranging from 0 to 10, with a mean of 5, there will be an equal number of measurements below 5 as above. Where data follows such a distribution (Figure 4.1a) it is considered to be parametric. However, data may be skewed to either the left or the right of

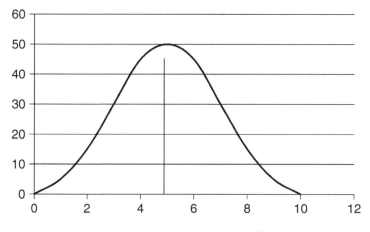

Figure 4.1a **Normal distribution curve (parametric data plotted on a graph)**

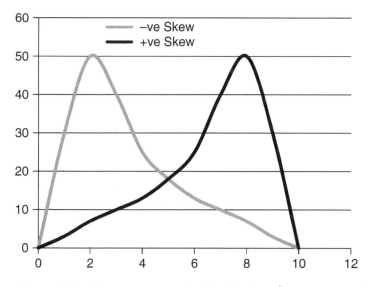

Figure 4.1b **Non-parametric distribution (non-parametric data skewed about a mean (average) point)**

the mean (Figure 4.1b), which means that the data is non-parametric. Non-parametric data would need to be analysed with different statistical tests from those used for parametric data. Quantitative analysis consists of a number of different tests that are based on mathematical formulae that enable you to judge if there is a difference between the observed measurements and those expected, or between two populations whose experiences differ by a single or multiple (measurable) variables.

This book is largely aimed at those undertaking educational and pedagogic research, so we cannot go into statistical analysis in great depth. Since it is very difficult to identify all the potential variables where individuals are concerned, quantitative studies are rarely considered appropriate in educational research. However, there are circumstances in which it is important to assess the validity of statistical analyses and so some basic understanding is important. We have included some relevant references and further reading at the end of the chapter to help you develop these skills.

Qualitative data

In recent years, confidence in the reliability of qualitative data and of its interpretation has grown because methods and methodologies have become more sophisticated and standardised. Qualitative data analysis describes and summarises the mass of words generated by interviews, focus groups, free-text response questionnaires or observational data.

Interpretation of qualitative data usually involves the identification (or application) of themes and an exploration of their relationships. It may also involve relating them to particular behaviours or ideas or to biographical characteristics of the respondents.

Analysis of qualitative data often informs changes to policy or practice, or sometimes interpretation may be sought for confusing findings from previous studies.

Ultimately, theory can be developed and tested using advanced analytical techniques.

Although methods of analysis can vary greatly, the following 11 steps are typical for qualitative data analysis:

1   Become familiar with the data through repeated reading, watching or listening as appropriate.

2   Acquire formal transcriptions of audio and audiovisual materials (you can do these yourself but someone who is trained to do this is likely to be much quicker and is unlikely to allow any personal bias

to interfere with the transcription of any difficult-to-understand segments).

3   Record observations, impressions and perceptions accurately and within a specific context.

4   Organise and index data for easy retrieval and identification.

5   Anonymise sensitive data.

6   Code (or index) data.

7   Identify themes (these should emerge from the data and would normally be a word or phrase used by participants).

8   Develop provisional categories (these are groups of themes that naturally belong together).

9   Explore relationships between categories.

10 Refine themes and categories.

11 Develop theory/interpret data and incorporate pre-existing knowledge to inform your conclusions.

Themes and categories

In the list above we described developing themes and categories from our data to help us organise and interpret it. Usually these themes will arise from the data itself (thematic analysis) but in some circumstances it may be relevant to use categories and themes you have already developed to test your theory in relation to a particular research question.

Practical task

Below are the responses from students to an open-ended question, *How do you know that the online information you use is valid and authoritative? Please give examples.* Try to identify the themes that emerge from this sample of qualitative data.

Often go through academic search engines (more often those at my home institution as opposed to at [university name]), use reference lists in assigned reading for coursework.

The professionalism of the webpage, the URL (if it ends in .org or not), through trusted search engines like the library, searching through the scholarly journal link on Google.

I use only published and credited works.

If it is a respected company or publication, one with lots of references, or is peer-reviewed it is normally pretty authoritative.

I only use university-approved online resources and books obtained at or through the university library. If I do use, for instance, wiki, it is only to help me find some light background information to help me do further research.

If I am going to use online content I make sure it is from a reputable source and not something like Wikipedia. At my home university there is an online library I can use that has all different web journals and publications that have been reviewed and are legitimate sources.

It depends on the ending of the URL. Also, it depends if they provide scholarly materials and can be traced back to another legitimate source.

Anything with a .org or .edu address online is normally valid. If I have any doubts I try to find another source or two that says the same thing. Other than that, I visit online journals and the like that my university has an account with or other websites that my professor recommends.

Academically trusted sites searched through Google Scholar.

Practical task continued

Usually teachers will give a list of sites to use or specific sites NOT to use. Usually if I am concerned I will check for an author and publication to make sure they are legitimate.

If the articles I'm using come from an academic database like JSTOR or from a news website like CNN.

Having identified the key themes, try to group them into categories.

When you have completed this exercise you will be able to see that reducing hundreds and even thousands of words into a few words or phrases that group together into even fewer categories helps you to interpret the key messages from the research you have undertaken. This analysis may be done through reading and re-reading a transcript and physically marking up the document. Alternatively, there are a number of tools such as mindmapping software (see the references and further reading section for examples) or qualitative data analysis software (e.g. NVivo, MAXQDA) that can help to automate the process. However, nothing can substitute for being very familiar with your raw data, which comes from extensive re-reading.

One of the greatest challenges with any data collection is ensuring that the approach you adopt is meaningful, relevant and unbiased by your own values, views and opinions.

Qualitative research methodologies

Many researchers and students struggle with the distinction between the terms 'method' and 'methodology'. A method is a process by which data is collected. In qualitative research this may include, amongst others, the processes of interviewing, observation or developing and administering a questionnaire. By contrast, methodology is a group of processes, usually underpinned by a theoretical concept that provides a framework within which your data is collected and interpreted. Examples of such methodology in qualitative research include phenomenology and ethnography. These are the methodologies most likely to be used by students of education along with action research, which may take a mixed methods approach. By this we mean that data may be obtained using both qualitative and quantitative methods. We are now going to take a brief look at these methodologies and some of the common data collection methods. Obviously we cannot do them complete justice in a book on critical thinking but there are recommendations for further reading and we will look at them briefly now.

Phenomenography

Phenomenography is a methodology *adapted for mapping the qualitatively different ways in which people experience, conceptualize, perceive, and understand various aspects of, and phenomena in, the world around them* (Marton, 1986, p31). This means that, undertaking a research study where we want to understand students' perceptions of their learning experience, our methodology would be phenomenographic. The methods we use to collect the data may include studying their writing or essays and studying transcriptions of focus groups or interviews. We can use a number of different methods to collect the data but they all need to focus on the experiences, perceptions and conceptions of those we are studying. Normally such data would be qualitative but we could obtain quantitative data by using a questionnaire that asks individuals to score their experiences (for example, on a scale of one to ten). However, translating qualitative, experiential/perception-based data on to a numerical scale has its problems in that individuals may struggle to assign a meaningful value. In phenomenography, the researcher is not part of the group but is an outside observer. This is distinct from the role of the researcher in ethnography.

Ethnography

Ethnography is defined as the descriptive study of a particular human society or group and usually consists of fieldwork, where the researcher (ethnographer) works amongst the people being studied for a period of time, striving to maintain a degree of objective detachment whilst being part of the community. An ethnographer usually cultivates close relationships with participants who can provide specific information on aspects of the way of life and behaviour in certain contexts. According to Spradley (1979), ethnography is *the work of describing a culture* (p3). He suggests that it is a useful tool for *understanding how other people see their experience* (piv) and emphasises that *rather than studying people, ethnography means learning from people* (p3).

While detailed written notes are the mainstay of ethnography, researchers may also use tape recorders, cameras or video recorders. Figure 4.2 describes a cycle which represents the process undertaken in ethnographic research.

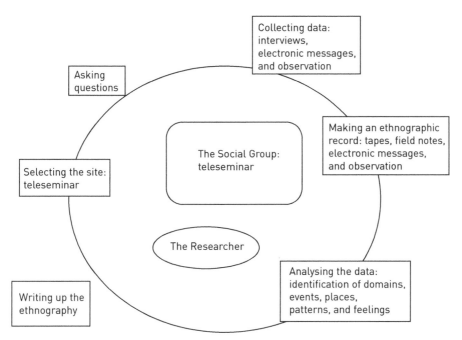

Figure 4.2 The ethnographic research cycle

Ethnographic research has broad implications for many fields, including education. Professional development evaluators and staff developers can use this approach to understand teachers' needs, experiences, viewpoints and goals. Such information can enable them to design useful and worthwhile programmes for teachers and ultimately improve student learning.

Action research

Action research is a methodological approach to understanding the impact of an intervention during a continuous process of change. It allows the researcher and participants to construct their own roles within the research process; these roles have the possibility of fluidity. If we accept that change is an ongoing process, action research involves iterative cycles of study and evaluation. The point at which the outcomes of any action research are published provides a snapshot in time of how change has influenced the question being studied; it does not represent an end. Thus action research is complex and multifaceted. Somekh (2006) provided a definition of action research based on eight methodological principles:

> *Action research integrates research and action in a series of flexible cycles*
> *involving, holistically rather than as separate steps: the collection of data*

about the topic of investigation; analysis and interpretation of those data; the planning and introduction of action strategies to bring about positive changes; and evaluation of those changes through further data collection, analysis and interpretation . . .

(Somekh, 2006, p6)

The methods used to collect the data may be qualitative or quantitative or a mixture of both. The difference is that, unlike phenomenography and ethnography, the researcher is neither an outside observer or integral member of the group – the researcher's role can change during the study depending on the nature of the change being explored.

Qualitative research methods

We shall now briefly look at some of the methods used in qualitative research and the fundamental rules you have to obey to ensure your data collection and analysis are sound and unbiased.

Interviewing

Interviewing is a method which allows you to gather information about an individual's perception, conception or experience of the topic upon which the interview focuses. It is a difficult technique to master and involves careful design of the questions and good listening skills.

Interviews may be structured – all the questions are preformulated to ensure you gather information about predefined issues, semistructured or unstructured. The latter two reduce the opportunity for researcher bias to influence the questions but carry with them the danger that the participant may not volunteer the information you are specifically seeking. These approaches however do allow participants to enunciate what is most important to them in relation to the issue being explored. Although we are talking about individuals, small groups (fewer than eight people and known as focus groups) may also be interviewed using a structured, semistructured or unstructured approach. The challenge with such groups lies in ensuring that all participants are enabled to make their contribution and that no one dominates the other members of the group.

As the interviewer, it is important to be an extremely good listener and not to interrupt a participant. It is also important to ensure that the participants feel free to speak their minds and this means that, wherever possible, the person conducting the interviews should not be in a position of power over the participants, e.g. a lecturer/teacher who is about to mark the participants' assessment artifacts.

The quality of your data is critical and so, whilst you may not wish to take notes during the interview process (to prevent interrupting the flow of the discussion), it is important to have clear electronic recordings of the session (either audio or audio and visual).

When developing questions for a structured or semistructured interview, it is important that the questions are phrased such that they do not force the participants to respond in the way that you wish them to. For example, you have introduced a new teaching method (role play) into your classes and you want to understand the students' perception of how helpful this approach has been in increasing their engagement with their lessons. You might ask:

Did the introduction of role play into the lessons help to increase your engagement with the subject you are studying?

With this question you are clearly telling the students what you hoped introducing role play would achieve – increased engagement with the lesson. What you want to know is what their perception was of it. Instead you might ask:

What did you think of the role play and why?

You can explore the details by follow-up questions that arise from their responses.

We have largely considered face-to-face interviews, which have the added advantage that you can see participants' body language. However, interviews are also carried out by phone and using more modern media such as instant messaging, synchronous discussion boards, Skype and other social media. Obviously the choice of media used depends on a number of variables, including the participants (and their degree of comfort with the media), their geographic locations and time/equipment constraints.

Surveys

Surveys are used to gain the opinions of a group of individuals on a particular topic. The instrument used to obtain survey data is the questionnaire. The design of such instruments is crucial to ensure that the responses are not biased or influenced by the researcher's own viewpoint. The basic principles of survey research are as follows.

1. Clearly identify your research question.

2. Clearly define the population you wish to survey and your sample size.

3. Decide on your method of data collection (online, by post, by phone).

4. Design your questionnaire and timetable.

5. Pilot your questionnaire with a small test population.

6. Distribute your questionnaire to your target population, giving reminders as per your timetable.

7. Collect and analyse your data.

Let's consider the question:

Do Christmas sales change shoppers' buying habits?

The target population will be people shopping during the Christmas sale period and it will be all those canvassed over the Christmas sale period.

The approach might be to have people with the questionnaire stopping shoppers and asking them the questions on your survey.

Now comes the tricky part: what questions are you going to ask? Remember after you collect the data and come to analyse it, you will not remember each individual who completed the questionnaire, so the answers to the questions need to give you all the information you require about the individuals themselves as well as their shopping habits. So you could ask the direct question:

Are the Christmas sales altering your shopping habits?

By asking this question you are telling your participants what it is you are trying to discover and the question requires only a yes or no answer. This will not tell you much.

Practical task

Take the scenario above and try to devise questions that will answer your research question without telling your participants what it is you are trying to discover. What other information do you need to know about the participants and their shopping habits and therefore what other questions do you need to ask? Remember it is important not to tell your participants the outcome for which you are hoping. Also remember that in a questionnaire you can ask a range of question types, including multiple choice, multiple response, forced ranking and open-ended.

Often questionnaire data is converted to numerical or quantitative data but it is important to consider how this may influence your outcomes. For example, using a Likert scale (a rating scale where people rate their preferences/experience on a scale – usually one to five, where one is worst and five is best), it is possible to get a numerical value for individuals' perceptions of how good a movie is or how satisfied they are with a service. However, it must be remembered that putting numerical values on perceptions relies upon individuals who will not only interpret things differently (depending on their previous experiences) but also how generous they are (or not) with their scoring. It is not uncommon for external examiners to complain about academic staff not using the full scoring scale when marking students' work – if a fail is 40 per cent and a first-class honours (in the UK) is 70 per cent, assessors may limit their marks between 25 per cent and 85 per cent – they don't use the full scale, despite having marking criteria that address 0–100 per cent. This is also true of people filling in Likert scale-type questionnaires. Often giving a top score means to individuals that the thing they are rating is perfect (obviously a difficult standard to attain and maintain). However, if we consider the Likert scale as a percentage, the grades imply the following:

1 = 0–20 per cent

2 = 21–40 per cent

3 = 41–60 per cent

4 = 61–80 per cent

5 = 81–100 per cent

As you can see, a score of 5 does not mean perfect but between 81 and 100 per cent of the time meets the highest possible standard.

As a generalisation, it might be said that when asking for individuals' views/perceptions/conceptions about something, it is much more reliable to allow them to give an open-ended response and to undertake qualitative data analysis than to rely on converting their perception into a quantitative value.

Thematic analysis

Audio, visual or textual data would normally be considered to be qualitative data. However, there are means by which such data can be converted to quantitative data and subjected to statistical analysis, usually associated with quantitative data. For example, the frequency of the use of certain words or phrases within two given populations may be compared statistically to demonstrate differences between them. However, this data can also be analysed qualitatively, examining both implicit and explicit ideas within the data giving rise to key codes, themes and subsequently categories. Analysis may include looking at which codes occur together. For example, in a study of hospital workers' perceptions of customer care, a common theme was 'lack of' and important codes were 'staff', 'time', 'resources' and 'leadership'. These codes all co-occurred within the theme 'lack of' (Clarke and Eales-Reynolds, 2013).

In grounded theory, codes, themes and categories developed from one study are applied to data derived from a second population where we are testing the theories developed from the first study which gave rise to the codes, themes and categories. It is a form of thematic analysis but is more complex in nature and attempts to generate theory in relation to the original research question.

Interpreting data

The interpretation of any data which you collect should be guided by your initial study hypothesis, theory or research question. Therefore, when you examine the data you must recognise the following issues:

- Data interpretation methods vary greatly depending on the theoretical focus (i.e. qualitative or quantitative research) and the research methodology you have followed.

- Ensure you understand relevant information on statistics. You should seek further advice for this step from computer package manuals (e.g. SPSS) and methodology books.

- The last step of data analysis consists of interpreting the findings to see whether they support your initial study hypotheses, theory or research questions.

Practical task

Below is an account of an incident which occurred during a student teacher's school-based training. This record is a piece of evidence and as such can be treated as part of the student's research data about the context of the student teacher's placement.

Entering the room with a great deal of noise, the child throws himself into his chair and folds his arms.

Teacher: Why have you been sent back?

Child: For nuffin'. I din't do nuffin'.

Teacher: You must have done something. Everyone says they didn't do anything.

Child: What's the poin' anyway? I 'ate school, you only ever get told off. I wish there weren't any school.

Teacher: But what would you do instead?

Child: Dunno.

Teacher: How would you earn a living? What would you do all day?

Child: I'd jus' play on me PlayStation and stuff.

Teacher: But if there wasn't school, how would a PlayStation have been invented? Where would you get a job to get the money to buy the games and the console?

Practical task continued

Child begins to fidget and smile.

Child: I dunno. They jus' would be there.

Consider the following:

- What information can you elicit from this piece of data?

- Is this a specific type of research data? What makes you think this?

- How would the data assist you to make judgements about the context of this placement and the child in particular?

Ethics

When designing research that involves the use of living species, we have to consider the ethics of such research. Research that involves the use of animals or human tissues (from persons in hospital or engaged in clinical trials) is highly regulated from an ethical perspective, usually at a national level. Research that involves the collection of perceptions or views of individuals (particularly action research) may be less well regulated from an ethical perspective. In some organisations, questionnaires and surveys are conducted without any consideration of ethics. However, it is always good practice to ensure that you are meeting basic ethical guidelines in regard to any form of data collection. Higher education institutions will have their own ethics committees and procedures for approval of different types of research. Many relating to teaching use the British Psychological Society ethical research guidance or some version thereof. As well as ethical approval from the appropriate body, you need to obtain informed consent from your participants. This involves them signing a document to say that they have read and understood the purpose of the study, how the data is to be collected, what will and will not be done with the data and give permission for their data to be used in that way. These should be signed before any data collection commences.

Summary of key points

In this chapter we have explored the differences between quantitative (positivist) and qualitative (interpretivist) data and the different methods one might use to collect the data and interpret it. We have also explored the differences between methodologies and methods. Finally we have touched upon the issue of ethics in gathering and using research data where human subjects are involved.

References and further reading

Charmaz, K (2006) *Constructing Grounded Theory: A practical guide through qualitative analysis.* London Sage Publications.

Clarke, C and Eales-Reynolds, L-J (2013) The human factors paradigm and health service employees' perceptions of customer care. *Nurse Education Today* (submitted).

Edwards, A and Talbot, R (1999) *The Hard-Pressed Researcher: A research handbook for the caring professions.* London: Longman.

Etherington, K (2004) *Becoming a Reflexive Researcher: Using our selves in research.* London: Jessica Kingsley.

Glaser, BG and Strauss, AL (1967) *The Discovery of Grounded Theory: Strategies for qualitative research.* New York: Aldine de Gruyter.

Langdridge, D and Hagger-Johnson, G (2009) *Introduction to Research Methods and Data Analysis,* 2nd edn. Harlow: Prentice Hall.

Marton, F (1986) Phenomenography: A research approach to investigating different understandings of reality. *Journal of Thought,* 21: 28–49.

Smith, K, Todd, M and Waldman, J (2009) *Doing your Undergraduate Social Science Dissertation.* New York: Routledge.

Somekh, B (2006) *Action Research: A methodology for change and development.* Maidenhead: Open University Press, McGraw-Hill Education.

Spradley, JP (1979) *The Ethnographic Interview.* New York: Holt, Rinehart, and Winston.

Strauss, A and Corbin, J (1998) *Basics of Qualitative Research Techniques and Procedures for Developing Grounded Theory*, 2nd edn. Thousand Oaks, CA: Sage Publications.

Viadero, D (1996) Researchers seek new road map for teaching. *Education Week*, XV: 9.

Websites

http://sourceforge.net/projects/freemind (accessed 12 February 2013): Free mindmapping software for data analysis and organisation.

www.bps.org.uk/what-we-do/ethics-standards/ethics-standards: British Psychological Society ethics pages.

www.wisemapping.com (accessed 12 February 2013): Free collaborative mindmapping tool for real-time collaboration. Limited sharing for free.

5. Developing your critical thinking skills: reading critically

Introduction

In this chapter we are going to look at the skills you need to practise, which will help you become a good critical thinker. Like every part of your body, your brain improves with exercise and two ways in which to do this are through reading and writing critically. We are going to look at how to read the resources you find, how to analyse and evaluate them and how to organise them.

Now, I suspect you are thinking, *I'm at university – I don't need to know how to read*. However, what we are talking about here is reading for a purpose. If you are to be a good critical thinker, you need to know how to find appropriate sources of information, how to judge their validity and how to determine if they are authoritative or not. So, in this chapter we are going to think about reading for a purpose.

Learning outcomes

By the end of this chapter you should know how to:

- decide which resources are relevant to your problem/issue/question;

- analyse what you read and gain from it the relevant information and understanding;

- record the process and information obtained for further analysis/ reference.

Reading for a purpose

We talked in Chapter 3 about finding resources, using various search tools and repositories and how your librarian can help you with these tasks. Now we are going to consider what we do with the resources we find in this way.

Practical task

Think of a question relating to a topic you wish to explore – it may be related to an assignment you have to perform or it may just be something in which you are interested, for example:

*   *How are numeracy skills taught in preschool?*

*   *How does gaining a BTEC impact on a student's chance to enter university?*

*   *What is authentic assessment and how is it used in higher education?*

You may think of any question you wish, but this will be your search question.

Now think of the keywords or search terms which you will use to help find relevant sources of information.

OK, that done, now let's start searching.

From your search results, choose five resources that you think are most important and write down what they are, why they are the most important and how you made that decision. We'll revisit this after the next section.

Identifying relevant resources

Once you have identified a set of resources through using your chosen search terms, you need to make a judgement about their relevance to your question: the authority of the source (i.e. has it been written by an enthusiastic amateur or someone who has an established reputation in the field?); the validity of the source's message or conclusions (i.e. is it based on false premises? Is the writer using rhetoric to persuade?); and the methods used to gain data/results/outcomes upon which the source is basing conclusions (i.e. are they appropriate and valid?).

This sounds daunting but there are some straightforward measures you can apply to help inform your judgement.

First of all, read the title of the article. Does it sound as though it may have a direct bearing on the research question you are trying to answer? If yes, then go further. If you are not sure, also carry on. You can eliminate sources at any stage of the following scheme.

Next, take a look at the abstract (if one is present). It will give you more information than the title alone and will help you to decide if the article is really relevant to your study. It should give you information about the study population, the methods used, the main outcomes and conclusions. For example, if you are only interested in ethnographic studies, then the methodological details in the abstract should allow you to include or eliminate the study.

Now look at the source itself. Some of the questions you might ask are as follows.

- Is it published by a reputable academic publisher?

- Is it published in an established peer-reviewed journal? (This means the journal has been around for some time and papers are sent to experts to review before being accepted.)

- Is it from another reputable source such as a professional body, university website or government website?

If none of the above applies, it doesn't mean you can't use it – you just have to be particularly thorough when analysing the resource. Sometimes, leading experts in their field may set up project websites or blogs to give the public instant access to their latest findings. So you also need to check the authors.

- Who are they?

- What are their credentials?

- Has their work been cited by others?

Again, coming up blank against all these queries does not stop you making your own judgement about a source of information. Just remember to look at how authors have derived their data.

- Has the resource been well cited (referred to) by others?

- Have they used appropriate/known methodologies?

- Have they used appropriate methods?

- If they have used tools such as questionnaires or interviews, have these been appropriately designed? Do you have access to them?

- Have they used appropriate tools to analyse their data?

- Are their conclusions logical and based on appropriate premises?

- Have they described the limitations of their study so that their conclusions can be appropriately interpreted?

Some or all of the above questions may be relevant to your evaluation of the literature. You can simplify the process by having a list of the questions and just ticking off which ones your resource satisfies. You then need to decide which are most important in your given circumstances and on the basis of this you can accept or reject the resource in relation to your study. For example, if you are doing a review of the literature to answer the question 'What is the current state of our knowledge in relation to the effectiveness of simulation in clinical education?', then there may be some very important secondary sources that would not meet all the criteria in relation to data collection but would still be important for your literature review if this were a well-cited (well-known) article in the field. (Primary sources of information are those that report the collection and interpretation of new data such as a research paper. Secondary sources of information are those that draw on the results of others to form novel interpretations and to generate new knowledge, e.g. review papers, reports, and provide their interpretation of the work of others which they cite (reference).)

When you have decided that the paper is relevant to your own study, then you need to record all the information (authors, title, year of publication, where published), preferably using a reference manager. (A reference manager may be as simple as a card index system or an Excel spreadsheet. However, sophisticated e-programs are available that automate much of the process of appropriate referencing and data management. Examples include Refworks, Endnote and Zotero.)

You should also take a note of the date you accessed the article, the search terms you used to find it and the search engine/databases you used. Finally you should take notes of the key information you are deriving from the article, why you think the work is valid and what element of your own argument this is supporting. If you think there are important quotes you will wish to use you should carefully take a note of them and the pages on which they occur. All of this information can be stored in a spreadsheet or in your reference manager software for future use. You may also want to make a note of the key premises/data on which any conclusions are based so that when you return to your notes, you will be able to judge the validity of any arguments presented. This is particularly important when you have contradictory evidence from two or more different sources. Once you have collected all this information you need to know how to put it together to support your views/arguments in relation to the question/issue you are seeking to address. We'll look at this in the next chapter.

Practical task

Now revisit your previous search and choose the five most important references using the approach described above. Has this changed your top five?

Summary of key points

One way to develop your critical thinking skills is to practise them. You can do this in a number of ways but one way is to search for information relevant to a particular problem or question you are addressing and to analyse and evaluate that information. It is important to question everything and because there is so much information out there, it is important to have a rubric/system that you can use to decide whether or not something is relevant to your problem/question and whether or not it is valid. You may like to do this by creating a pro-forma checklist that you can complete for each article or information source you evaluate.

Another way to develop your critical thinking skills is through writing. Visualisation of your thoughts and argumentation laid out in a structured way can help you see how your skills are progressing. We shall address this in the next chapter.

References and further reading

Browne, MN and Keeley, SM (2009) *Asking the Right Questions: A guide to critical thinking*. Harlow: Pearson Education.

Cottrell, S (2005) *Critical Thinking Skills*. Basingstoke: Palgrave Macmillan.

Metcalfe, M (2006) *Reading Critically at University*. London: Sage Study Skills.

Websites

http://endnote.com (accessed 31 January 2013).

www.refworks.com (accessed 31 January 2013).

www.zotero.org (accessed 31 January 2013 (freeware)).

6. Developing critical thinking through writing

Introduction

In earlier chapters we have explored the skills and attributes required by a good critical thinker. In order to develop these skills it is necessary to practise them and this can be done through well-planned active learning and purposefully designed communication such as writing and presenting. In his book, Bean (2011) discusses how well-designed writing activities around a relevant problem can develop students' critical thinking as well as their engagement in the discipline and their professional expertise.

Learning outcomes

Having worked through this chapter you should be better able to understand:

- why writing helps you to develop critical thinking skills;

- how assessments can be designed to encourage the development of these skills.

The nature of your assignment impacts your ability to practise critical thinking skills

No matter what form your assignment/assessment task takes, it is likely that you will be required to provide some form of written work. In mathematics, students are often penalised for not showing how they've worked out the problem. This is the mathematical equivalent of showing how they have thought it through, and used their existing knowledge and understanding to arrive at their conclusion. Of course, in creative disciplines, assessment artifacts may take the form of performance or design and production of specific materials and the way in which you can demonstrate your critical thinking skills may be very different.

As with all skills, critical thinking skills are developed through practice – whether this be verbally in discussion and argumentation with others, through writing or mentally rehearsing your argumentation. What you write and the extent to which you can practise and demonstrate your critical thinking skills will depend upon the expected outcome of the assignment and how it is designed. For example,

> *Write an essay on modern educational theories.*

This encourages you to reproduce the information from any relevant lectures you may have had and to include information you may have obtained from textbooks and any other reading you may have undertaken. This would help you practise your descriptive skills but does not encourage you to reflect on where the gaps in your knowledge might be. It also may lead to you practising your skills of information gathering (although if a lecture on the topic has been part of a course, students will often only use these notes and possibly the additional recommended reading). It is important that to be a critical thinker you must demonstrate a rational (logical) approach to such information gathering that involves selectivity based on the exercise of judgement as to the validity and relevance of the information to the subject under consideration. The basic acquisition of knowledge and its memorisation or reproduction without interpretation do not constitute critical thinking and may lead to the problem of plagiarism, as we discussed in an earlier chapter.

Writing for an assignment

Before you start any assignment, you need to be clear about your focus. At university it is expected that you will think critically about the requirements of the assignment by exploring the learning outcomes for the assignment/module. Learning outcomes are what it is expected that you will be able to do at the end of a module and that you have to be able to demonstrate through some form of assessment. This may be through coursework or examination. Often you will be given formative assessment – this is work that does not count towards your mark, but will help you develop your skills through practice and feedback from your lecturer/tutor. This feedback should help you to identify where you need to do more work so that you are better prepared to demonstrate the skills you have learned.

How do you know what is expected of you when you start to write an assignment? The following suggestions are essential if you are to understand any assignment brief.

- Read your programme/course/module (unit) handbooks – these should tell you the learning outcomes associated with the module and even with the assignment you are undertaking.

- Look at the key skills you are required to develop within your programme as a whole and your module and then determine which skills you are expected to demonstrate in the particular assignment brief.

There will be advice available online or in physical resources (either in the handbooks or on your course/module site online) to help you develop your academic writing skills. Some disciplines have particular ways of structuring certain types of assessment (e.g. science and law) and even have a disciplinary language that is expected. For example, in science it is usual to write in the third person; instead of *I did this* a scientist would write *This was done*.

Assignments should be designed to allow you to demonstrate the learning outcomes expected for the module. In order to ensure that you know which of the learning outcomes any particular assignment is addressing, you need to analyse exactly what the assignment is requiring you to do. Assignment descriptions or questions will contain direction words that help you identify what is expected from you. Verbs are crucial in telling you how you should answer the question and it is vital that you understand these as they help you to formulate analysis and discussion in your assignments. Table 6.1 gives some definitions, but there are many more in study guides.

You may be given a list of factors (or criteria) to consider in your assignment guidelines. Do not assume this is a ready-made plan. Sometimes the list is not in any particular order and is only there to guide you. Try cutting the list up and moving the points around to help you make a structured plan. If in doubt, check with your tutor. You may be given the assessment criteria that will be used to evaluate your work. These provide clear guidance as to the knowledge, understanding and skills expected to be exhibited in your work.

Vocabulary	Explanations
Account for	Explain, give reasons for
Analyse	Break an issue or problem into parts and discuss each part objectively, giving a variety of arguments and evidence
Argue	Support or reject a position by presenting reasons and evidence for and against each position
Comment on	Use evidence to explain why something is, or is not, important
Compare	Show the way things are alike and explain why
Contrast	Show the way things are not alike and explain why
Critically	Objectively give your judgement about the subject of the assessment based on relevant and valid information you have gathered
Define	Give the precise meaning of something or offer different meanings for the same thing
Discuss	Present reasoned arguments based on relevant premises looking at all sides of the issue(s) and arrive at a conclusion
Evaluate	Decide whether something (the focus of the question) is important or not important, relevant or irrelevant or effective or ineffective. Give examples and evidence for your reasons
Explain	Based on your own knowledge, demonstrate your understanding of the issue in clear language to enable understanding in others
Illustrate	Use clear examples and/or case studies to contribute to an explanation
Outline	Give the main features, principles, events, etc.

Table 6.1 **Some definitions of examples of vocabulary used in assignment titles and examination questions (adapted from Assignment Guidance, Edgehill University Faculty of Education)**

Practical task

The following is an assignment brief:

Critically evaluate the evidence for and against the efficacy of the lecture as a means to promote learning, using examples from practice to illustrate your answer.

First of all identify the words that are telling you what they want you to do; you might want to highlight these with a particular colour. In the example above these would be:

critically evaluate and *illustrate*

Next, you could highlight other key words that set the context for the assignment. These include:

the evidence; *efficacy of the lecture*; *promote learning*; and *examples from practice*

Next brainstorm your ideas (either on paper or by using an online mindmapping package) to help you map your ideas (e.g. define the term 'lecture', list the theories that relate to the promotion of learning). An example of a basic mindmap is shown in Figure 6.1. This should help you keep track of your thoughts and ideas and structure your response.

It may help you to understand the question if you rewrite it in your own words (e.g. *Examine in a critical manner the evidence for and against the idea that lectures encourage learning. Use practical examples to support your argument*).

Start by breaking the assignment brief down asking further questions, e.g. What do we mean by learning? What other forms of pedagogy promote learning? How do lectures promote learning?

(Figure 6.1 shows how you might use a mindmap to track your thinking when analysing what an assignment question asks you to do. In **bold type** are words and phrases from the question itself. In *italics* are your thoughts about the way in which you might get started. As you work through the process of information gathering, you can add thoughts and quotes from the resources you have found.)

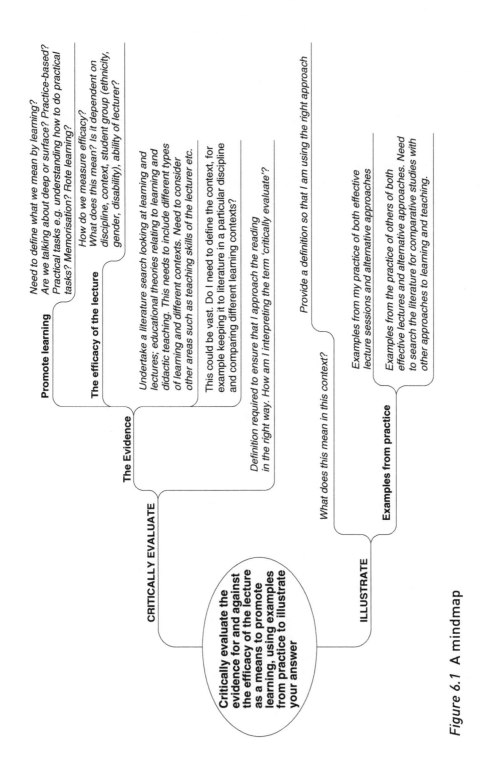

Figure 6.1 A mindmap

Planning your assignments

As with many things, planning is vital to doing something successfully. It helps to keep you on track and prevents you going off at a tangent. You may write a lot but if it does not address the focus of your assignment, you won't get any points for it. These are some simple steps you can follow.

- Break down the question.

- Brainstorm (using some form of mindmapping).

- Read your course notes and any additional recommended reading.

- Do your extra research (this helps to make the difference between a good and an excellent outcome).

- Make an outline plan.

- Allocate words to each section. (Don't try at this stage to get a perfect draft down on paper. Just trying to organise your thoughts and ideas in the different sections of your outline can really help you get started with your writing.)

- Polish your work to produce a draft (you may be able to discuss this with your tutor at this stage).

- Redraft and edit.

- Proofread.

Worked example

Below is a worked example which demonstrates the stages a student undertook when answering the following assignment.

Critically examine the education professional's role in promoting language diversity in the classroom. In particular, consider the issues related to the immersion/bilingualism debate. Provide a detailed analysis of how children who have English as an additional language can be supported in their learning, making reference to a child or group of children you have worked with in school or nursery.

Here are four steps that helped the student in thinking through her answer. This is one way of approaching the task (not the only way), and it is applicable to any discipline.

1. Identify your initial view and why you hold it. Writing out your initial ideas will help clarify your thoughts. To do this you must read critically in order to identify and explore the evidence within the literature. For example:

(a) You would start from your own experiences and knowledge base such as any classroom experiences you may have had. Below are the student's initial thoughts as she started this assignment:

Last year I worked in a nursery which had a large proportion of children who had been in the country for less than a year. Because their English was so limited and they struggled with what they were asked to do, I thought it would have been a good idea to withdraw these children from working and playing with their peers and be given small group tuition in English.

(b) Below is a selection of resources which the student read and accessed to increase knowledge and understanding of the central issue:

Crosse, K (2007) *Introducing English as an Additional Language to Young Children: A practical handbook*. London: Heinemann.

Editorial Team Teachernet, last updated May 2007. Available online at **www.education.gov.uk/schools/pupilsupport/inclusionandlearner support/eal/a0076755/english-as-an-additional-language** (accessed March 2013).

Scott, C (2008) *Teaching Children English as an Additional Language*. London: Taylor & Francis.

2. Seek other views and more evidence. Make sure you examine all sides, especially those that are contrary to your ideas or what you have observed in, for example, your practice. Consult people who have expertise in the topic. For example:

After reading Gregory (1997), I realised the disadvantages in withdrawing children from their English-speaking peers. Instead I now believe that it would be much better to focus on speaking and listening learning experiences which included all the children to enable the non-English speakers to learn from their peers as well as adults.

3. Evaluate the evidence using valid criteria, which will be determined by your framework of evaluation. Construct a chart with points that are in agreement and disagreement, then compare these with your initial view. Present evidence to support your discussion/argument. For example:

You will now need to read some specific texts to help you reflect on the appropriateness of your initial views of *speaking and listening experiences which would enable the non-English speakers to learn from their peers as well as their teachers*, such as:

Editorial Team Teachernet, last updated May 2007. Available online at: **www.education.gov.uk/schools/pupilsupport/inclusionandlearnersupport/ eal/a0076755/english-as-an-additional-language** (accessed March 2013).

Gregory, E (1997) *One Child, Many Worlds: Early learning in multicultural communities*. London: David Fulton.

Hall, D (1995) *Assessing the Needs of Bilingual Pupils: Living in two languages*. London: David Fulton.

Judge, BC (2003) Chapter 9 in Crawford, K (ed) *Contemporary Issues in Education: An introduction*. Dereham: Peter Francis.

Porter, B (2004) *Understanding Each Other: Supporting children with English as an additional language (EAL) in early years settings*. Chester: Cheshire County Council.

4. Construct a balanced argument. Your challenge is to develop a response you consider to be the most logical in the light of the evidence available to you. This will be a synthesis of the information you have researched from multiple perspectives and your initial ideas on the issue.

Online assessments and critical thinking

Today it is quite common for students to be required to keep a blog or for groups of students to create a wiki. This may be for assessment purposes, as a reflective diary or for personal and professional development. Writing in a blog or wiki still requires the author to set the context and to develop arguments and draw conclusions. However, this process may be fragmented over a number of entries or indeed modified by other contributors.

When writing a blog it is sensible to review your earlier entries occasionally and see whether your viewpoint, position or conclusions have changed as you have explored more information sources. Through the agency of reflection you can then update your position and perspective. The joy of these tools is that it allows you (and your assessor(s)) to see the generation and development of your skills.

A wiki can be more problematic from the perspective of presenting your personal viewpoint because others are allowed to change the material. However, it does enable you to engage in a form of argumentation with others and demonstrate your ability (or the power of your argument) to persuade others of the validity of your position. Again, you and your assessors can see the genesis of the work.

Summary of key points

In order to develop your critical thinking skills you need to practise them and this can be achieved through assessment, particularly through writing. It allows you to explore your understanding of an issue, practise your ability to explain it, search for sources that may expand your existing knowledge, analyse and evaluate their contribution and help you to present reasoned arguments and arrive at a judgement on, or personal perception of, the issue. When writing your assignments, the following prompts will help your construction.

- Define the problem carefully and completely.

- Explore all sides of an issue.

- Be willing to change position when shown valid reasons and evidence that persuade you to do so.

- Seek alternative solutions in an attempt to choose the best solution.

- Realise that the best is not the same for everyone.

- Remain open to others' values and opinions.

- Question and compare conflicting interpretations of data.

- Evaluate conclusions.

Having completed a draft of your assignment it is important to re-examine it to determine if you have demonstrated the required learning outcomes. This process of review and reflection can also enhance your learning. We will consider how you can analyse your own writing in the next chapter.

References and further reading

Bean, JC (2011) *Engaging Ideas: The professor's guide to integrating writing, critical thinking, and active learning in the classroom*, 2nd edn. San Francisco, CA: Jossey-Bass.

Beveridge, AN (1997) Teaching your students to think reflectively: the case for reflective journals. *Teaching in Higher Education*, 2: 33–43.

Crosse, K (2007) *Introducing English as an Additional Language to Young Children: A practical handbook*. Oxford: Heinemann.

DfES (1999) *All our Futures: Creativity, culture and education*. London: HMSO.

DfES Central Advisory Council for Education (1967) *Children and their Primary Schools* ('The Plowden Report'). London: HMSO.

Gregory, E (1997) *One Child, Many Worlds: Early learning in multicultural communities*. London: David Fulton.

Hall, D (1995) *Assessing the Needs of Bilingual Pupils: Living in two languages*. London: David Fulton.

Judge, BC (2003) Chapter 9, in Crawford, K (ed) *Contemporary Issues in Education: An introduction*. Dereham: Peter Francis.

Porter, B (2004) *Understanding Each Other: Supporting children with English as an additional language (EAL) in early years settings*. Chester: Cheshire County Council.

Scott, C (2008) *Teaching Children English as an Additional Language*. London: Taylor & Francis.

Websites

www.education.gov.uk/schools/pupilsupport/inclusionandlearnersupport/ eal/a0076755/english-as-an-additional-language (accessed 4 February 2013): Resources relating to teaching English as an additional language.

7. Analysing your own writing

Introduction

In previous chapters we have looked at how your critical thinking can be developed through improving your information literacy skills and in practising your writing. This chapter looks at the process of reviewing your own writing and how analysing it can be used as an aid to learning. This chapter guides you through checking the level of your criticality. It shows you how this criticality may be built into your writing.

Learning outcomes

Having worked through this chapter you should be better able to:

- reflect through writing (i.e. learn through writing and write reflectively);

- review the style and structure of your writing;

- consider the importance of the clerical tasks of editing and checking.

Thinking about your thinking . . . reflecting on your reflections . . . analysing your analysis.

Reviewing your written work

One of the things we are always told is *make sure you check what you have written*. How many times have we heard that and what sense have we made of that statement? How often do you re-read what you have written, not just to check for spelling and grammatical errors but also to ensure that the point of view you are trying to communicate is really clear?

Reviewing your own writing at a simple level is easy and involves:

- re-reading sentences to check that they make sense;

- reading paragraphs before moving to the next section to ensure continuity;

- reading from the start after a break to get yourself back into the flow of the writing.

However, as discussed in the previous chapter, writing helps to develop your critical thinking skills and you need to ensure that what you have written demonstrates these. Therefore it is necessary to exercise these skills in analysing your own writing in order to ensure that your writing has captured your higher-level thinking. This means that you must be:

- willing to question your own personal views;

- open to the ideas and views of others;

- questioning the interpretation and conclusions of others (remember, just because it is in the public domain does not mean that it is correct or valid);

- able to make (positive and negative) judgements;

- able to explore the implications of the evidence/data;

- self-confident enough to present your own interpretation of the information you have gathered;

- honest in facing your own biases/prejudices;

- flexible in considering alternatives and opinions;

- willing to reconsider and revise views where critical reflection suggests that change is warranted.

Analysing your work in this way may reveal deficiencies in your argumentation or areas that need further clarification or substantiation in the form of evidence. This evidence may come from your own personal practice/experiences. Metacognition or self-reflection is often helped by the requirement to keep a personal development plan/portfolio and many students are encouraged to keep reflective journals; recording their experiences, observations, perceptions and learning. These journals can be invaluable resources for aiding the development of critical thinking and self-confidence and may provide sources of information to support your argumentation. This is known as self-referencing.

Worked example

The more familiar form of self-referencing is the straightforward use of quotations from a learning journal or a teaching file in a formal essay. In this worked example a student teacher writes about her class teacher's use of one child with good English as an Additional Language (EAL) skills to support another child newly arrived in the class from Pakistan.

My teacher decided to seat Child A next to a bright child, Child B, who also originated from Pakistan and spoke both Urdu and English very well. It was explained to me that Child B could help with translating in the classroom as well as providing personal support to Child A throughout the school. As a new arrival, Child A needed to learn EAL as quickly as possible.

Following feedback from the assistant on Child A's English language development, my teacher started to give Child A the same set work as children in Wave 3 of the Primary National Strategy . . .

I, however, was concerned about . . . the onus on Child B to support Child A.

Looking back to notes in my journal (16/10/08) I noted:

Child B speaks Urdu and has been helping Child A a lot but I sense that Child B is really getting fed up with it now as Child B has less time for their own work.

The impact of this extra responsibility was further evident when I came to mark Child B's report writing task for literacy. Child B is one of the top ability writers but this was not reflected in their work. I decided to speak to them . . . they then confided that they had not been able to concentrate as Child A was occupying a significant amount of their time asking questions.

The writer took a brief quote from her journal and then expanded on it in her essay, providing additional evidence to back up her view.

Suppose now that we consider how the student might take a more critical approach. She might have written that her 'sense' of something in the quotation *but I sense that Child B is really getting fed up* was initially left without the evidence that led to her supposition. The paragraph that follows does provide this evidence, but we do not know for certain what created the sense in the first place. To link the two would have provided a stronger logical flow to the writing. A critical style of writing might be as follows:

> *Child B speaks Urdu and has been helping Child A a lot, but I sense that Child B is really getting fed up with it now as Child B has less time for their own work.*

> *I believe the 'sense' that I had was not merely intuitive but was evidenced when I marked Child B's writing. Child B is one of the top ability writers but this was not reflected in their work.*

This follow-up is critical in the sense of revealing more or making more evident (not in the sense of finding fault or shortcomings).

Reflection

The term 'reflection' will be familiar to many students, particularly those who are studying subjects that involve professional practice. Frequently you will be required to reflect on your experiences as a means of learning. You will probably be familiar with the adage that a reflective practitioner learns from every experience, but the non-reflective practitioner will do the same things over and over again.

How does reflection relate to analysis? Quite simply, analysis is part of the reflective process, but it is also a term that is applicable in other contexts. To start with, the word 'reflect' implies looking back. It will require thinking back to place yourself in the learning situation. It requires imagination to conjure up the detail. Considered in a reflective moment, the possible anxiety of the situation can be confronted and thought through. The term was first used in an educational context by the American academic Dewey (1933). The ideas were developed by Boud et al. (1985, pp26–31) in the form:

- *returning to experience* – recalling or detailing important events;

- *attending to feelings* – using helpful feelings and removing or managing obstructive ones;

- *evaluating experience* – re-examining experience in the light of one's existing knowledge.

Reflective task

Think of an example of how you have reflected on a learning experience. Consider the following aspects:

- Were you able to describe the situation accurately with enough detail such that you could identify what was effective and what didn't work so well?

- Were you able to identify precisely any problems or strategies to improve your learning/understanding/practice?

- Did you discuss the problems with anyone? If so, consider what you learned from that discussion. Were you able to incorporate what others said into your reflection on the experience?

- What form did the reflection take? Did you write it down and if not, what might the process of writing have added to the value of your reflection?

- Have you used the learning gained from the reflective process? Were you able to refine your understanding further? If so, how?

There are many different interpretations of the term 'reflection', often related to particular disciplines and the way reflection is used. For example, scientists would probably refer to 'critical self-evaluation' rather than reflection. This difference in semantics is common across disciplines (even the term 'critical thinking' defies cross-disciplinary consensus about the skills and attributes it includes). The important issue is not the label that is used, but the learning that occurs from a particular process.

If you are not familiar with reflection, it is a common mistake merely to write a descriptive account of an event or experience. However, learning comes from deeper consideration, analysis and evaluation. A simple prompt for one new to 'reflection' is as follows.

- What? Give a clear description of the events and processes in relation to a particular circumstance. Set out the context of your learning and perhaps what the expected outcomes were. What emotions did you experience or how did it make you feel?

- So what? Explore the meaning and impact of your observations in the light of your current knowledge and that which is accessible elsewhere. How has this experience impacted on your knowledge/understanding/ practice/values? Was it valid and meaningful and if so, in what way? Did it have impact on you, your practice and on others?

- Now what? What can you do with this new knowledge/understanding? What relevance does it have to you as a developing professional? How might you use it to influence or inform the subject knowledge base, others or professional practice?

Reflective task

Look at an essay or journal in which you have been required to reflect. Consider how you have addressed each of the three categories of reflection and whether there is a good balance in emphasis between them. Note that description is a necessary part of the process of revisiting the examined situation, but it needs to be selective and accurate. Good, relevant detail is valuable and feelings may offer important insights.

Levels of reflectiveness

A set of descriptions of levels of reflectiveness is useful when self-assessing written work that is reflective in character. Kember et al. (2008, pp369–79) propose four graded categories for assessing reflectiveness: (1) habitual action; (2) understanding; (3) reflection; and (4) critical reflection.

Habitual action

Expert practitioners do this in routine situations which they have met many times before. Students may follow rigidly a procedure that they have been taught (the student may then provide material in an essay without any sense of the meaning).

Understanding

In this case the student will demonstrate understanding of the technique or strategy but will have difficulty in applying it because it remains a theoretical concept. In writing, the explanation will show understanding but not how it might be used in practice. It has not become part of the student's working practice.

Reflection

Reflection requires students to relate concepts and ideas to their own experience. In written work, ideas will be illustrated appropriately with examples from the student's own practice.

Critical reflection

Critical reflection implies a change or transformation of perspective. When practice has become habitual this is more challenging. Students new to the practice will be more open to the possibility of change. This requires students to recognise their own assumptions and to review them critically.

Reflective task

Look at the same piece of reflective writing as in the last task and decide, as objectively as possible, which reflectiveness level it matches. Your judgement should be on a best-fit basis. You may find it helpful to isolate paragraphs and analyse them separately.

Reviewing style and writing structure

Some readers may have developed confidence in structuring their writing. However, this section addresses those who are uncertain and offers approaches to reviewing how writing may be put together. As mentioned before, the expected structure of any written work will vary across disciplines. However, as a student your work will normally be framed by an introduction and a conclusion. The following section looks at the essential features of these structural elements.

The introduction

Generally, an introduction briefly sets out what you intend to cover in your written work. In essays that have a very non-specific brief that requires you to select the focus, it becomes necessary to clarify your choice. The title *A critical analysis of the potential for interdisciplinary teaching and learning in foundation subjects* would be followed by an instruction to select one or a group of subjects as a focus for the discussion. The introduction would then outline why such subjects were chosen, which cross-curricular themes are to be included and a reference to any general findings that might follow. There might well be an expectation that the student's own experience of teaching or experiencing the subjects being taught would be analysed and subjected to questioning.

In response to the instruction: *Submit a piece of writing reflecting your personal response to the way an aspect of one of the tasks carried out in school has raised questions about your own practice,* the following student clarifies not only the fact that her topic is cultural inclusion, but also from where she is drawing her examples and the fact that she is adopting a critical approach:

> *Children from ethnic minority backgrounds now form a tenth of the pupil population (Mohan et al., 2001, p1). Given this fact, I realised the significance of inclusive practices and the embracing of all cultures during my first primary school placement. What I was not prepared for was the introduction of a seven-year-old boy into my Year 3 class who had just moved from Pakistan with no prior exposure to the English language.*

> *In this piece of writing I will analyse my class teacher's practice, both positive and less so, in handling this situation . . . I will then reflect on my own response to this challenge in respect of my own teaching and investigate what I could have done and what I can do later in my placement to improve learning and teaching for the child.*

Not all essay titles leave room for customising in this way. *Analyse how ICT can support creative learning and teaching* is a straightforward instruction. It lends itself to an initial discussion of the issues raised and illustration by example from the literature, but it is not encouraging reflection and therefore the inclusion of personal experiences. Also, some disciplines, particularly those with a positivist, scientific basis, do not encourage the use of personal pronouns and so therefore tend not to encourage the inclusion of examples of self-reflection. However, that does not mean that students should avoid providing their own conclusions about the matter under consideration.

The conclusion

The generally accepted pattern for a conclusion is that it summarises the main points raised in the essay. The danger with this is that it if the conclusion does not say or reveal anything new from the accumulation of the insights already discussed it will be superfluous. In the following example, in response to the instruction, *With specific reference to a particular literacy lesson which you have taught, identify and discuss two strengths and two growth points*, the student successfully makes one new, more general point not explicitly stated in the essay itself. In the essay the student had described situations that were leading towards this broader point, such as, *My lesson did not follow the typical Literacy Hour structure; however I do not feel that for this task it was necessary. I still incorporated many objectives from the [Literacy Strategy].* However, she held back from drawing the main conclusion, which is as follows:

> *The National Literacy Strategy (NLS) is only recommended. It is a guide to how we the teachers can provide our children with the opportunity to reach the required targets set by the National Curriculum. It will not always be appropriate to follow exactly the structure of the Literacy Hour. It is an excellent starting point, however, and truly has, in my opinion '. . . substantially raised literacy standards among primary school children by encouraging teachers to reach reading and writing in ways which have not been widely used in England' (Beard, 2000, p245). It is a matter of exercising our own discretion to decide the techniques that will aid the children most successfully to reach their full potential.*
> (Lauren Smith, unpublished 2004)

Structuring the main content of the essay

If your university programme is vocational, it is primarily concerned with developing practice. The purpose of academic study in relation to this practice is to encourage a reflective and informed approach. The brief of an essay will commonly expect any theoretical idea to be illustrated by examples from your own experience. If this is done appropriately (i.e. it illustrates the theoretical point fully, not vaguely or in part), it will demonstrate that you are operating at a reflective level. In some forms of writing you may be expected to discuss a theoretical point, back it with reference to relevant literature and then illustrate it with reference to your own experience. Here a student first writes theoretically about creativity and then gives an example of her own experience:

> *The Plowden Report said over forty years ago: 'At the heart of the educational process lies the child.' If the child is truly to be central, creativity and originality must be paramount, otherwise the child is the passive recipient of information . . .*

> *Immediately on entering the area of my first placement school it was obvious that there is encouragement of learning through play . . . There is an area on the corridor outside the classrooms where books and other activities linked to current topics can be found.*
> (Christine Everett, unpublished 2008)

These would be reversed in another form of essay in which students are being encouraged to develop their own ideas and theories first. The example could be analysed as an example of an environment that encouraged active and independent learning. Only then would writers refer to other authorities in the literature that they had been reading.

Clerical tasks of editing and checking

You will not need reminding that any written work must be read through and checked for minor errors, fluency and sense. Unfortunately, too often feedback on students' work states that *there are many spelling and grammatical errors* and that *it would benefit from careful and critical reading.* Artists will sometimes spend a period of time up close to their canvas working on detail. It is only when the artist stands back that it is clear that the colour balance has been upset or the angle of the nose on a portrait is wrong because the part could not be assessed in relation to the whole canvas when viewed close up. The same is true for writing. If we have spent some time on writing something we often are pleased to see the end of it and don't want to revisit. However, take a step back (get a cup of coffee or something) and then return to the work, reading it through from start to finish. This will help you to judge whether your argument really does hold together. Also take care with paragraphing, to ensure that each paragraph has a central theme which is clear from the beginning.

Then there should be attention to the clerical tasks. After a spell check from the computer, another readthrough is necessary because spell checkers will only pick up mistakes (e.g. mak instead of make) and not words that have been used incorrectly (e.g. *the letter was form* rather than *the letter was from*). Only after these important checks can you consider your work ready for submission.

Summary of key points

In order to demonstrate your learning through written work, it is necessary for you to identify what is expected of you and that you have clearly evidenced this in your writing. To do this you need to set the context of your work (the introduction), provide evidence of your thinking on the subject through quoting the work of others and using your own experiences to contribute to your understanding, provide valid argumentation based on evidence-based premises that support your viewpoint and then draw your conclusions. Depending upon your discipline and the type of artifact you are required to produce (essay, blog, scientific report, etc.) the language used, the structure and the tone will vary, but the need to demonstrate criticality will be common.

Make sure your essay introduction lets the reader know what the main themes of your writing are. Reserve an interesting feature or general point for the conclusion. Make sure you allow time for the important clerical tasks of editing and checking. Lack of care makes your work appear unprofessional. Poorly constructed sentences, spelling and grammatical errors can make your work difficult to read and therefore affect the flow of your discussion or commentary. It impacts on the ability of the assessor to judge the level of competence you are demonstrating in relation to the learning outcomes that are being assessed. This brings us nicely to the issue of assessing criticality. We have already explored the challenge of defining precisely what skills and attributes comprise critical thinking and therefore an even greater challenge is recognising the demonstration of these skills in written work and then assessing them. We shall address this in the next chapter.

References and further reading

Beard, R (2000) *Developing Writing 3–13*. London: Hodder and Stoughton.

Boud, D, Keogh, R and Walker, D (1985) *Reflection: Turning experience into learning*. London: Kogan.

Dewey, J (1933) *How We Think*. New York: D.C. Heath.

Kember, D, McKay, J, Sinclair, K and Kam Yuet Wong, F (2008) A four category scheme for coding and assessing the level of reflection in written work. *Assessment and Evaluation in Higher Education*, 33: 369–379.

Mohan, B, Leung, C and Davidson, C (2001) *English as a Second Language in the Mainstream: Teaching, learning and identity*. London: Longman, pp. 200–201.

8. Assessing criticality

Introduction

In this chapter we will look at ways in which we need to use our own critical thinking skills when assessing or evaluating the work of others. We will also be looking at how we can recognise evidence of critical thinking in students' written work.

We have looked at how we can evaluate our own criticality but actually assigning a mark to the work of others is more problematic because we have our own perceptions of what we expect from the work. It is important to remember that if we are expecting students to be critical in their writing we are not just assessing their 'knowledge', i.e. the information they have obtained, but also how they have synthesised that information and used it to inform their own arguments and conclusions.

Learning outcomes

At the end of this chapter you should be able to:

- use/develop an appropriate rubric to support you in assessing the work of others;

- recognise the demonstration of critical thinking skills within the work of others;

- assess critical thinking in the work of others confidently.

Assessing critically

It is usual when setting an assessment to design it so that it encourages student learning and enables them to demonstrate the expected learning outcomes of their study. Employers are crying out for employees who can think critically and, as we have seen throughout this book, it is possible to develop the relevant skills and attributes, particularly through developing information literacy skills and writing critically. In order to assess such skills it is necessary to:

- devise appropriate assessment tasks that encourage these activities;

- understand exactly what it is you are looking for in the finished work.

Reflective task

Which of the following essay titles is most likely to encourage the development of critical thinking skills in students and why?

Write a critical essay on Great Expectations.

Describe the plot of Great Expectations.

Compare and contrast the characters of Magwitch and Pip in Great Expectations.

The exercise above is very simplistic but it illustrates the importance of understanding exactly what students are required to demonstrate in their assessment. This will be defined by the learning outcomes that the assignment is addressing but also the particular skills the students are required to develop. For example, it would be expected that, regardless of the topic, students need to demonstrate some or all of the skills associated with critical thinking – the further developed they are in their learning, the more they should be able to demonstrate this.

This raises the issue of the importance of considering critical thinking development across the curriculum and identifying where the opportunities lie for students to develop them. In the first chapter you will remember that we said that critical thinking comprises a number of different skills and attributes and that, rather than a linear developmental path, it may be that, depending on the question or challenge, some skills are used more frequently than others. So, for example, it is important that you know how to recognise what is important and be able to describe and explain a situation clearly before you analyse and interpret it. For this reason it may be that, earlier on in your study cycle, these are the skills that are preferentially developed. Therefore, at this stage, it would be these skills that any assessment task should be addressing.

Once an assessment has been designed, it is necessary for the assessor to understand what it is that is being evaluated and how it will be graded. It is also really important for students to understand this, so that they can focus their learning through the assessment on the key skills they should be developing. This may sound easy and is, if all you are looking for is the recollection of facts such as in science or the recall of historical events. However, this becomes much more difficult where demonstration of the full range of critical thinking skills is required.

Recognising criticality

If the expectation is that students will be demonstrating some or all of the skills associated with critical thinking in their assignment outputs, then the assignment task needs to be designed to allow them to do so. However, assuming this is the case, then the assessor (which may be you) needs to be able to recognise these skills in the student's writing. It is also important for students to be able to recognise that they are fulfilling the requirements of an assessment by demonstrating criticality. So can we identify criticality in writing?

Reflective task

This exercise includes three pieces of writing. You should read each one and try to decide which skills are being demonstrated in the writing. Try to identify the passage that you consider demonstrates the strongest critical thinking.

An incident occurred during a science practical class which resulted in a student being injured. An investigation of the incident required the staff present to write a report of the incident. These reports would form the basis for a decision about whether or not a formal investigation would be required.

The following passages were provided by: (1) a graduate teaching assistant; (2) the technician; and (3) the lecturer.

1. I was acting as a teaching assistant for the practical. The lecturer gave me a handout the day before and asked if I understood it and if I had any questions. It seemed quite straightforward and I had done the same

practical myself when an undergraduate so felt I knew what the students had to do. The class had been running for about an hour and most of the students were working to schedule. I was circulating around the room to answer any questions and check that the students were doing the practical correctly. Suddenly there was a loud cry and I rushed to where a group of students had gathered. A female student was clutching her hand and I could see blood everywhere. I shouted for the lecturer who came and took over. The technician told the other students to go back to their workstations and continue with their work. I resumed circulating the room. I don't know what happened to the student and I couldn't attend the accident debrief.

2. The incident occurred on September 13th, in the first practical class on module 101, introductory biology. The practical was a classic one in which students are required to cut equal-length strips of potato and place them in each one of four tubes containing different concentrations of sterile saline solution. The tubes are left at room temperature for an hour and the students are then required to remove them and measure their lengths. From this data they are required to deduce information about the relative strengths of the different solutions. The solutions were evaluated using the Control of Substances Hazardous to Health (COSHH) regulations. No special measures were required for their use in the experiment. All students were given a copy of the form and asked to sign that they had read and understood what to do in the event of a spillage. All students were asked to wear white coats and plastic gloves. After a demonstration by the lecturer, the students commenced the practical working in pairs. A graduate teaching assistant was circulating round the room but was not really paying much attention to what the students were doing. I noticed one group of older students who were not giving careful attention to their actions. I asked them to be more careful but they did not seem to take any notice. Analysing this situation I felt that it offered considerable potential risk and as a result I was particularly watching them when one student nudged the other as they were about to cut the potato. The scalpel slipped and cut the student's finger which proceeded to bleed profusely. I was on the other side of the bench and shouted to the student to put pressure on the wound and called the lecturer to the bench. The lecturer seemed to know what to do and I judged it best for me to let him deal with the wound whilst I cleaned up the blood – mindful of the regulations governing the clean-up of blood spillages for which no HIV or hepatitis status is known. I covered the blood with absorbent paper and soaked it in disinfectant (Virkon, an antiviral). Having assured the safe cleansing of the workstation according to current health and safety guidelines, I told the graduate teaching assistant to allow the students back to their stations, cautioning them about the need to be responsible when using scalpels. I had noticed that the lecturer was not wearing gloves when

dealing with the student and discreetly took him a pair since I judged he also could be at risk. On reflection, I think it would have been better to have the students using only one or two stations for cutting the potatoes where they could have been under close supervision and prevented from larking around. Also, raising students' awareness about the risk of blood-transmitted diseases in a laboratory would be a good preventive measure against such an accident happening again.

3. The practical class during which the incident occurred was part of the introductory biology module for which I am module leader and have been so for five years. This particular practical class has run for all five of those years and we have never had an incident like this before. The experiments were designed to help students apply their theoretical knowledge of osmosis to interpreting the outcomes of what they did in the laboratory. The class comprised 20 students who were working in pairs. The students self-selected their partners. Of the 20 students, 12 were female, 8 male and 13 were from an ethnic minority. Also present in the class were an experienced technician, who had run the previous practicals, and worked at the university for more than ten years, and a graduate teaching assistant who had never assisted in a practical class before. Students were required to cut up a potato into strips and to put it into tubes containing different concentration salt solutions. After incubating them at room temperature for a set period of time, the students had to remove the potato strips and measure their lengths using the provided measure. They then had to interpret this data (in the context of their knowledge of osmosis) and draw conclusions about the relative concentrations of the salt solutions. I started the practical with a demonstration and stressed that the students had to be careful with the scalpels they were using to cut the potato. I did not see the incident but, when called by the technician, I arrived and quickly applied pressure to the wound. Having trained as a first aider, I applied my knowledge in dealing with the incident. I asked the student to wash the finger under clean running water and applied a sterile gauze to the cut with pressure. After some time the bleeding stopped and I applied a plaster to the cut. I decided at this time that it was safe to allow the student to return to the practical to watch the final stages but not to take part as I did not want the student to risk reopening the wound. I have run this practical on numerous previous occasions and this was the first accident that has occurred. However, the risk of injury using scalpels is quite high and so I had ensured that I had read the health and safety literature in preparing the practical to reduce this risk. On reflection, it might have been better either to have the strips pre-cut or to have had all students doing the cutting in one place with constant supervision.

What did you do in the exercise above to decide which report was demonstrating greater critical thinking? Did you use the criteria we discussed in Chapter 1, i.e. the skills that someone needs to demonstrate to be considered a good critical thinker? Table 8.1 shows each of the criteria (skills) and explains how they might be evidenced in the reports.

Reflective task

Using Table 8.1 to support you, re-examine your conclusion from the exercise above (considering the three pieces of writing). Do you still arrive at the same result? If not, why not?

Criterion-based assessment

Assessing critical thinking is not a standardised process across any education system. In the North American continent and in some disciplines, criterion-based rubrics are used to assess the demonstration of critical thinking skills. One example of such a rubric may be found here: **http://npiis.hodges.edu/IE/documents/forms/Holistic_Critical_Thinking_Scoring_Rubric.pdf** and was designed by Facione and Facione (1994, 2009) who carried out the study discussed in Chapter 1 of this book. The authors quite rightly point out that critical thinking skills are unlikely to be assessed in isolation; students may also be expected to demonstrate subject knowledge, professional competency and practical applicability, and so it is important that the assessors consider performance against all learning outcomes and not just those relating to critical thinking. There is another issue in that all rubrics are open to interpretation and so there is a need to ensure that all assessors interpret them in the same way. For example, at Washington State University a rubric was used that listed a set of dimensions and raters were asked to assess student demonstration of these on a scale from one to six (Rutz et al., 2012). It is important that raters all used the score of, for example, four in an equivalent way. In order to assure this concordance, considerable staff development and training were given to the raters. In addition, it is often the practice, particularly in professional, practice-based subjects, that more than one individual rates a student's performance against a scale and that interrater reliability is determined for the whole group. This highlights some of the issues and challenges in rating something over which there is no general consensus;

Criterion	Application
Interpretation	This is the demonstration of your understanding of what you are reading or observing. So, in the example above, in order to demonstrate the individual's perception of the occurrence, it is necessary to give a detailed description of what exactly occurred from each person's perspective. This demonstrates what they understood to have occurred
Analysis	This is the detailed examination of the elements that comprise a question or issue allowing you to try to find meaning in the information or data. So, in the example above, what are the key observations made by each individual? What do they tell you about the incident? What in their reports tells you what happened?
Evaluation	Having decided on your information (in this example, the perceptions of the incident from the three witnesses), you need to evaluate it. Do all witnesses concur or are there contradictions? It so, which is likely to be more reliable and why? Do the individuals give supporting evidence to suggest that their report is more reliable or accurate?
Inference	Inference is the part of the critical thinking process where we start to consolidate our own knowledge with that which we have found, in order to create new understanding. In the incident above, as a result of your evaluation and analysis, what do you infer happened? If you are used to working in such environments, you may have previous knowledge which can help you to interpret what you have learned from the statements but be careful not to let it bias your interpretation
Explanation	To explain your reasoning clearly and coherently you must be adept at making your thinking plain and comprehensible to your audience. Having undertaken the previous steps, you should now be in a position to make your judgement or conclusion about the incident and to give your recommendations. It is important to provide clear premises for the basis of your conclusions
Metacognition	One of the challenges of critical thinking is the requirement to be self-aware, to understand how our own experiences and biases may influence any conclusion we may draw. In this instance it would be important to ensure that no personal biases towards the individuals concerned affect your judgement or recommendations

Table 8.1 Assessing critical thinking using the Facione and Facione (2007) criteria

different assessors and those in different disciplines will have distinct ideas as to which skills demonstrate critical thinking.

A range of other frameworks or rubrics is identified in the reference and further reading section of this chapter and we would encourage you to explore these and see which fit with your own discipline and practice.

Assessing critical thinking in blogs and wikis

A further challenge exists in assessing or evaluating critical thinking skills demonstrated through written work using the media of blogs and/or wikis. Blogs provide an opportunity to observe how a student's critical thinking skills have developed over a period of time but may not provide a summative example of the culmination of this development. It is important therefore in designing assessments based on blogs that students are required to incorporate a reflective approach to reviewing their progress and development of their ideas. This helps to develop their understanding of precisely what critical thinking is and how they can demonstrate it.

Wikis are often used for group learning and projects. As an assessor it is more difficult to track an individual student's development; it requires successive versions of the wiki to be explored and individual students' contributions to be looked at. Again, requiring students to post a final reflective critical evaluation of the development of their knowledge and understanding through the process of collaborative learning will help embed their learning and develop their comprehension of exactly what critical thinking comprises.

Use of standardised critical thinking tests

There are a number of recognised and standardised tests that are designed to assess an individual's critical thinking skills. They are used in higher education and in industry to determine the level of an individual's skill but also if candidates' skills might be appropriate to the organisation they are joining. These tests are sometimes used before and after an intervention designed to enhance a student's critical thinking skills to judge if the intervention has been successful. The two most well-known tests are the Watson-Glaser Critical Thinking Appraisal (which tests the skills of inference, recognition of assumptions, deduction, interpretation and evaluation of arguments) and the California Critical Thinking Skills test (which is based upon the work of Facione, as discussed in Chapter 1). These tests variously comprise a series of questions and exercises that ultimately result in a summary score which is compared to a large norm population (i.e. the results of a large number of individuals who have previously taken the test and fit a particular demographic). This gives a measure of one's ability in critical thinking. Since these tests are not contextualised in a particular discipline, they are thought to demonstrate more clearly your ability to translate your disciplinary learning into other contexts. It is important to remember, however, that such tests are interpretive and they all have their limitations.

Summary of key points

Assessing critical thinking requires us to understand what it is we are looking for and how the student might evidence that within a disciplinary context. There are a number of frameworks or rubrics that may help in the task but it is important to determine if those in existence are applicable in your discipline or need modifying. It is also important to ensure that all those involved in assessment have a common understanding of how to score the evidence provided in a piece of work. One way to mitigate against variability between assessors is to have more than one assessor and determine inter- and intra-rater reliability. Finally there are standardised tests that can be used to assess critical thinking skills in a non-disciplinary context but these can only be interpreted by trained assessors and are subject to the same riders in relation to reliability.

References and further reading

Angelo, TA (1995) Classroom assessment for critical thinking. *Teaching of Psychology*, 22: 6–7.

Bell, A, Kelton, J, McDonagh, N, Mladenovic, R and Morrison, K (2011) A critical evaluation of the usefulness of a coding scheme to categorise levels of reflective thinking. *Assessment and Evaluation in Higher Education*, 36: 797–815.

Facione, PA and Facione, NC (1994, 2009) *How to Use the Holistic Critical Thinking Scoring Rubric: Insight assessment.* San Jose, CA: California Academic Press.

Facione, PA and Facione, NC (2007) Talking critical thinking. *Change: The Magazine of Higher Learning*, 39(2): 38–45.

Fry, H, Ketteridge, S and Marshall, S (2000) *A Handbook for Teaching and Learning in Higher Education*. London: Kogan Page.

Rutz, C, Condon, W, Iverson, ER, Manduca, CA and Willett, G (2012) Faculty professional development and student learning: what is the relationship? *Change: The Magazine of Higher Learning*, 44: 40–47.

Websites

http://faculty.education.illinois.edu/rhennis/tewctet/Ennis-Weir_Merged.pdf (accessed 4 February 2013): This is the Ennis-Weir critical thinking essay test.

http://npiis.hodges.edu/IE/documents/forms/Holistic_Critical_Thinking_Scoring_Rubric.pdf (accessed 25 January 2013): Rubric designed by Facione and Facione for assessing critical thinking skills.

https://www.barstandardsboard.org.uk/media/1344440/watsonglaser_form_ab_example_questions.pdf (accessed 4 February 2013): Examples of the types of questions in the Watson-Glaser critical thinking test.

www.insightassessment.com/Products/Critical-Thinking-Skills-Tests/California-Critical-Thinking-Skills-Test-CCTST (accessed 4 February 2013): California Critical Thinking Skills test based on the research of Facione and Facione.

9. A critical thinking community

Introduction

In this chapter we will explore the ways in which you can develop your critical thinking skills in collaboration with others. A range of particular skills is required in order to work effectively in a collaborative way. Some of these skills you will need to bring to the experience, while others you will develop as you become more experienced in the approach.

Learning outcomes

Having worked through this chapter you should be able to:

- recognise the value of working with others to develop your thinking;

- make use of a range of skills for working collaboratively;

- contribute to the learning of others.

Working collaboratively

In his review Angelo states: *There is wide agreement that college students learn more and better when they (a) are actively engaged and personally invested, (b) receive comprehensible and timely feedback, and (c) work cooperatively with peers and teachers* (Angelo, 1995, p1).

However, Cooper states that *despite numerous studies in relation to cooperative learning, the evidence of how this is causally related to improved critical thinking in students is problematic* (Cooper, 1995). This probably reflects the general lack of consensus of what critical thinking actually comprises and also that it is not necessarily general practice to assess the development of critical thinking skills specifically. However, one might infer that discussing a problem with a group of individuals will give a range of perspectives (based on differing background knowledge) that may give greater clarity of understanding, resulting in enhanced interpretation and synthesis of the information.

Many programmes of study will include opportunities for learning in collaboration with others, rather than in isolation. Students may be set investigative tasks which need to be done as a group, or they will be asked to communicate their work through a group presentation. For many students this may be a new experience. It takes time to move from studying by oneself to working with others. Clearly there will be tensions as well as opportunities, and it is worth considering how you will handle these tensions in order to establish the best atmosphere for everyone's learning.

Reflective task

Reflect back on your educational journey thus far.

How many opportunities have you had to work collaboratively?

Do you feel you work well within a group? If so, why?

Have you found collaborative working to be effective? If so, in what way? How has the experience differed to that if you had tackled the work alone?

Do you have reservations about working collaboratively? If so, what are they and why?

Learning communities

Learning collaboratively makes use of an embedded human trait which recognises that we are dependent on one another and need to work as a team to be more effective. None of us can expect to know everything there is to know about one subject or possess all the skills required to fulfil a task. Each of us brings our own life experiences, values and perspectives to each endeavour.

Within an educational context, working collaboratively recognises that we are all working within a similar framework. It is likely that we will all be tackling similar tasks. Therefore, it makes sense for us to consider challenges together. The group members with whom we are working will bring their individual prior experiences, learning and culture. Some members may have specialised in particular aspects of their field or may come from different educational or cultural backgrounds and bring with them different perspectives as a result of this. Working collaboratively offers the opportunity for each of us to share these experiences and expertise, and learn from those of others in the group.

Practical task

Think about a particular problem or question related to your field of study. Now make a list of the experiences, knowledge, perceptions, skills, values and attitudes that you are able to bring to a collaborative study group.

Identify when and where you developed these attributes.

What do you think are the key gaps that others might fill?

The challenges of working collaboratively

Sometimes you will hear people referred to as 'good team workers'. This usually indicates that they are comfortable working collaboratively in a particular environment. However, working in this way is not without its challenges. Some of us are indeed comfortable with collaboration, but some of us are less confident with it. We may be used to relying on ourselves to address tasks and prefer to work independently. This can make us resistant to collaboration as we are unsure that we can trust other members of the group in the way that we trust ourselves. Trust is absolutely key to working in a group. You have to trust that the other members will play their part and they must trust you to do likewise.

Some of the advantages of working collaboratively can also be seen as disadvantages. For example, each of us seeing things from a different perspective also means that we may not agree on certain matters. Also, sharing the workload may be an advantage but only if all members of the group do what is expected of them in the given timeframe. It is important to be aware of these challenges as you embark on collaborative work so that potential difficulties can be anticipated and, hopefully, minimised.

Practical task

Divide a page in half and consider the advantages and disadvantages of working collaboratively. Discuss with a colleague how you might overcome the challenges.

Now we are going to consider some approaches to collaborative learning.

Action learning sets

'Action learning' and 'action learning sets' or ALS are terms that have been widely used in the learning and teaching literature. ALS has in recent years achieved considerable popularity, often used in continuing professional development activities.

The concept of ALS is attributed to Reg Revans (1998), who developed it as a way of improving shared learning within organisations. It is considered to be a valuable way of developing a collaborative approach in which peers can share their own learning and contribute to the learning of others.

There are several ways of operating ALS, depending on the desired outcomes. For the purposes of this chapter, ALS will offer a way for students to develop their critical thinking skills in collaboration with others who are working on similar projects. The aim of the ALS is to develop each individual's thinking so that they can put something into practice more effectively. Thinking and action are thus equal partners. The group meets on a regular basis throughout an identified period, perhaps three months, to share their work, thoughts and problems.

ALS involve participants in re-evaluating their experiences through the process of sharing them with others. Each member offers their perceptions and views on a particular topic or challenge to the rest of the group. Informed by their prior academic and/or experiential learning, the requirement to articulate their knowledge and understanding necessitates that individuals engage their critical thinking skills. This process helps to consolidate their sense making of their various knowledge sources. The group is invited to respond to each member's input through the process of appreciative enquiry – asking stimulating questions that encourage the original contributor to think in different ways about the topic or challenge and thereby stimulating greater understanding and insight. For example: What are the principal causes of famine in Africa? Health professionals may say it is due to the depleted workforce due to endemic AIDS reducing the number of young healthy male adults. However, an educationalist may believe it is due to a lack of accessible education to provide the expertise to develop agriculture and so may ask the originator to consider the role of education in the cause of famine.

ALS encourage us to be open to new ways of seeing and interpreting our experiences, to welcome the perspective of others and value the challenges to our own assumptions. They can help us to clarify our thinking and narrow down the real concerns that underpin our interest in an area.

Establishing an action learning set

ALS usually comprise between four and seven people. These numbers are considered to be big enough to ensure contributions from a variety of perspectives but are not so large as to inhibit people or prevent them from having the opportunity to contribute. The participants usually have a common interest; group members are familiar with the context in which each other is operating.

There are a number of things that need to be considered when establishing ALS – some practical and some more fundamental.

- Should set members know each other well or be complete strangers?

- Should attributes such as gender, nationality and age be standardised within a group or not?

- Are all participants able to meet at a particular time and place?

- Does the meeting need to be face to face or could participants join electronically?

- Should the groups be self-selecting or assigned?

(**Reflective task**)

Think of a particular problem that you wish to address through the use of ALS and then consider all the issues that impact on designing the membership of the set.

What are the advantages and disadvantages of each alternative?

Operational considerations

At the outset, the ALS members need to identify what they hope to achieve by working together. This will depend on whether the group has a shared concern or whether their formation is based on specific criteria, such as friendship groups or common professional backgrounds.

A shared concern can be more valuable as the members are likely to be pondering the same issues, reading similar material and trying out similar strategies in the practice context. However, the strength of ALS where each member is tackling a different challenge is that the group members can bring a different perspective to the interpretation and solution.

The ALS members need to understand the expectations of all participants and to agree on how they plan to operate, when and where they will meet and what rules they need to follow in order to work effectively. Early in the process the group might wish to develop their own guidelines for working together. They might also consider what they will do if a member of the group does not follow the guidelines. For example, will the other group members confront the member or will an individual be nominated to do this? Indeed, the group may decide to allocate certain roles to each participant. Some ALS have a facilitator who is external to the group and some are self-facilitating. Some groups may nominate a scribe or a discussion leader. Such roles also need to be clarified, and could be rotated around the group over the weeks.

Once the aims and rules of the ALS have been established, members should be encouraged to share their initial areas of interest or concern (preparation for this might be a requirement in advance of meeting). During the meeting, ALS members may be given the opportunity to share their issue or concern to establish the range of issues to be addressed by the group. Meetings may include:

- reviewing notes taken at the previous meeting;

- sharing written work generated by the group;

- focusing on one or more members' work;

- discussing an issue that is of concern to the whole group;

- questioning of some or all members' work;

- giving verbal/written feedback to members;

- documenting the meeting;

- generating action points to bring to the next meeting;

- agreeing on the focus of the next meeting.

At the end of a meeting, members should agree personal tasks in preparation for the next meeting.

Key skills for effective ALS

We have talked about the role of effective communication in ALS. However, equally important are effective listening skills, the development of which is crucial to this process. This means resisting the temptation to interrupt, try to anticipate what a group member will say next or jump in with your own anecdote. It means using active listening skills which attempt to hear not only what the person is saying, but what lies behind the words. It also means allowing silent spaces to enable speakers to think and giving them enough uninterrupted time to finish what they want to say.

Questioning skills are also critical to effective ALS. Questioning might involve asking for clarification, unpacking assumptions and challenging contradictions or faulty reasoning. It should not involve 'putting words into someone's mouth'. For example, *So, what you mean is XXXX, isn't it?* This is giving the group your interpretation of what the person is saying and shuts down further interaction. Open questions, which allow respondents to elaborate on points and share their perspective, are preferable to such closed questions. Practising appreciative inquiry is a good approach. (Appreciative inquiry is a way of looking at what is going right to solve problems, rather than on exploring what is going wrong and causing the problem.) This means that questions are phrased to elicit a positive approach and do not dwell on what has gone wrong.

Examples of the type of open questions members might ask include the following.

- *Could you just clarify (explain a bit more) what you mean by . . .?*

- *What do you mean by . . .?, Why is that important? or How is that significant?*

- *How do you define the term . . .?*

- *Can you give us an example of . . .?*

- *Is it possible that there might be a different interpretation of . . .?*

- *How do you know that . . .? or What evidence is there for . . .?*

- *If this is the case, what might need to be done?*

Members must avoid trying to attribute their own views and interpretations to the speaker. They should avoid:

- shifting the focus to their own areas of interest;

- saying what they would have done in a similar situation;

- attempting to give answers to the questions;

- offering suggestions of how they may operate in future;

- entering into an argument in order to exert power.

The individuals who are presenting to the rest of the group also have skills to learn. It is important that they:

- speak as clearly and concisely as possible;

- avoid anecdotal evidence;

- are prepared to substantiate claims;

- do not assume a shared understanding of terms and concepts;

- avoid giving simple explanations of events;

- do not dwell on past experiences which can no longer be changed;

- anticipate future practice;

- are open to alternative suggestions that they have not previously considered.

Another important attribute that ALS members should exhibit is emotional intelligence. They need to consider the values, beliefs and feelings of the other group members in making their presentations. One way to judge the impact of what you are saying on group members (either as a presenter or questioner) is to observe their body language. Research demonstrates that the signals we share through body language play a critical role in communication. We subconsciously pick up on body language and it can make us defensive or upset, emotions which prevent us from really hearing the information being communicated.

At the end of an ALS meeting, members should feel that they:

- have been able to contribute to others' learning and in turn have learnt something themselves;

- are confident in their own expertise and curious about the next stage of their investigation;

- are clear about the expectations of the next meeting and what they need to do to prepare for it.

Online collaborative learning

In this age of the internet and mobile and flexible learning, younger learners are quite comfortable with engaging with others virtually. This has the advantage that individuals can learn in their own environments with resources to hand and, with asynchronous collaboration, can contribute at a time and place to suit themselves. However, such e-collaboration also requires other skill sets and considerable facilitation. For example, we have discussed how important communication skills are in collaborative working. Online, we lose two of our major communication routes – body language and tone of voice. For example, read the following interchange between two people:

Wow, I love that outfit.

Which one?

That one over there in the window of that charity shop.

Now, body language (smiling, laughing, relaxed) and voice intonation (sarcastic, joking) would tell you that your friend was not being serious about the two-piece, thick woollen suit in the window. However, the same statement being made by someone who has stopped in her tracks and shows tension in her body (excitement) and whose voice intonation implies excitement and enthusiasm would tell you that your friend was really serious (and probably needed some fashion advice!).

This is a simplistic example but it demonstrates how the same situation can be interpreted in different ways given our ability to read body language and interpret intonation. How can we do that online?

Practical task

A message on an asynchronous discussion board:

Message 1

George,

I don't think you are right in your assumptions about the question. In my opinion you are all wrong and your conclusions are stupid. It's obvious that you haven't understood the whole concept and this cannot be considered to be a contribution to the discussion.

Message 2

Dear George,

Thank you so much for your contribution to the discussion. It really made me think about my own interpretation and conclusions and question them again. That was really helpful. However, I think perhaps I did not explain the concept fully enough which has led to you missing one of the key premises on which the argument is based. [Goes on to describe the concept in alternative, clear terms.] I hope this helps and perhaps you would now like to consider it further and come back to us.

Consider both of the messages above. Identify what is right and wrong about the way in which each message is composed.

What do you think the impact of each message will be on George?

It is important to remember that, because asynchronous discussion only relies on the written word, it is easy for it to be misinterpreted. Starting a message with no salutation such as Hi! or Dear XXXX can appear terse and rude and will immediately put your reader into a less than receptive mood. Making a statement that could be misinterpreted is also very easy. Sometimes people use emoticons or caveats, e.g. <grin>, to tell their reader the tone in which the statement is made. However, be wary of overdoing it.

It is really important in asynchronous discussion that you write clearly and use words that are likely to be understood by all. If you have to use technical terms or jargon, explain them. The same goes for acronyms.

Forming online groups

One of the things that online group work does not allow easily is the socialisation that occurs when a face-to-face group meets. This is really important because the members have got to form opinions of each other and learn to trust each other. In order to facilitate this it is often useful (if possible) to get the online groups together face to face at the beginning, so this initial socialisation can take place. This may be physically or virtually through the use of Skype, FaceTime or tele/video conferencing. If not, then the early stages of forming an online group must be to engage members in exercises that encourage them to share some personal information with each other so that they can demonstrate trust and start to build the relationships. This requires skilled facilitation such that the facilitator does not interfere with the coherence of the group but does ensure participation and engagement. This type of online group facilitation is clearly described by Salmon (2004).

Working online with others

We have talked above about some of the challenges in working collaboratively online. There are many other things we have to consider in that individuals must be aware of the attitudes and beliefs of their coworkers so that they do not offend them inadvertently. Sometimes these things are hard to discern and so there has evolved a set of 'rules' for successful engagement online. This relates not only to collaborative working but also to any sort of online communication. The rules are known as 'netiquette' and it is always useful to use this to inform the 'rules' for any online collaborative working group. A useful link for netiquette is provided in the references and further reading section at the end of this chapter.

Summary of key points

Working collaboratively makes demands of, and furthers, your critical thinking skills. Working in this way has its advantages and challenges – the challenges are multiplied when the collaborative working is online. A clear structure is needed for collaborative working, both face to face and online. It can give us the confidence to explore our own critical skills through encountering those of others and gives us the opportunity to contribute to the learning of others. When working in collaboration participants should always demonstrate emotional intelligence, being aware of their collaborators' beliefs, values and emotions.

References and further reading

Angelo, TA (1995) Classroom assessment for critical thinking. *Teaching of Psychology*, 22: 6–7.

Cooper, JL (1995) Cooperative learning and critical thinking. *Teaching of Psychology*, 22: 7–9.

McGill, I and Beaty, A (2000) *Action Learning: A guide for professional management and educational development,* 2nd edn. London: Kogan Page.

O'Neil, VJ and Marsick, J (2007) *Understanding Action Learning*. New York: AMACOM.

Revans, R (1998) *ABC of Action Learning,* 3rd edn. London: Lemos and Crane.

Salmon, G (2004) *E-tivities: The key to active online learning*. London: Kogan Page.

Websites

www.jiscmail.ac.uk/policyandsecurity/etiquette.html (accessed 4 February 2013): This is the Joint Information Systems Committee link that gives the basic rules of netiquette – a guide to ensuring you do not offend or cause misunderstanding when working online.

10. Critical thinking in the professional context

Introduction

A significant part of any course of study which is designed to prepare students for a specific profession will usually involve periods of study in a work context. This experiential learning provides you with knowledge derived from your own experiences and reactions to the environment. This knowledge may contradict that which you have gained in your academic studies and you will need to be able to analyse and evaluate your experience critically in order to judge how this impacts on your existing knowledge. The synthesis of the two (your existing knowledge and that derived from experience) enhances your understanding of your discipline and allows you to apply the integrated knowledge to your practice.

Placements are designed to give you experience of being a member of your profession and to enable you to put into practice some of the knowledge and understanding you have gained from your academic studies. Although each work-based placement serves a similar purpose and works towards similar goals, you will quickly discover that they are all very different and have their own distinctive features. The reasons for these differences are many and varied, and it is important that you recognise these differences and analyse why they exist so that you can judge the value and validity of the experiential knowledge you are gaining and how that impacts on your knowledge construction and the application of that knowledge in your practice.

Learning outcomes

Having worked through this chapter you should be better able to:

- analyse the features of a placement context critically;

- develop your critical thinking skills in relation to placement contexts;

- use a critically reflective approach to identify how you might modify your practice to meet the unique needs of each practice environment.

The significance of context for professional development

Any professional programme of study must recognise that individuals' performances are substantially affected by the context in which they operate. No amount of classroom study can ever prepare a student for the infinite variety of experiences they may come across in the work context. In earlier chapters we have looked at how a critical thinker must question everything. In the work context, students often do not feel empowered to question authority. However, it is important to do so, because only by questioning and exercising our critical thinking skills can we learn from the experiential knowledge of peers. Sometimes, there may be the temptation for students on professional programmes to ask to be told 'the right way' to do something or the 'gold standard'. The truth is that 'the right way' is contextually dependent. In a work context anything we do or learn must take into account the particular demands, priorities, opportunities and limitations offered by a particular place.

The significance of context is related to the opportunities you will have to develop certain aspects of your professional practice. First of all you need to reflect upon your learning to date and identify those required professional competencies that you need to develop. Being aware of your own strengths, weaknesses and values allows you to analyse critically each new placement in the context of those aspects of professional practice that you need to develop. Such consideration of context also offers a significant strategy for learning. As you gather information about the context, you build a bank of data that you can analyse at a later time to track how you are relating and responding to that context and what you have learned.

This rich data can then be evaluated in the light of your other studies (e.g. reading, university lectures and seminars and conversations with colleagues). Your analysis can help you to synthesise the different data sources to build a more useful picture of your professional work.

Practical task

Review your own professional development thus far.

Which areas do you feel you have made progress in?

In which areas do you feel you need further development or experience?

Make a list of your next five priorities for development. Consider how context might affect your ability to address these areas.

For example:

Priority 1: In order to be able to meet my learning outcomes I need to understand how my academic learning can be translated into real-world learning (e.g. a biomedical scientist who has learnt the theory behind professional practice needs to understand how it is applied in a live clinical laboratory).

Importance of context: Since my discipline covers a range of areas, I need to experience a range of different workplace contexts to be able to demonstrate the transferability of my learning (e.g. a bacteriology laboratory, virology laboratory, etc.).

The process of contextual analysis

In order to make the best use of contextual analysis, it is important to plan for it as carefully as you might plan for any other aspect of your learning. This means being alert to information from the beginning of your time in the particular placement and having a strategy to process this information.

Initial analysis

Before you even arrive at your new placement setting, you will begin to build a picture of what it will be like. The very name of the organisation or institution will provide indicators of the setting. For example, you can assume that the Hospital for Rheumatic Diseases is a specialist clinical centre and a school called St Matthews C of E has a Church of England foundation and is likely to have Christianity as a reference point. You may also begin to formulate some view of the place because of its location (e.g. inner city or rural).

Information about the context may also be available from external sources, such as local authorities, professional organisations, the Department for Business, Innovation and Skills, the National Health Service or even family and friends who have some knowledge of it. It is useful to gather this data as a starting point for getting to know the context. Try looking at the organisation's website in order to gather information about its ethos and ethics. However, we must exercise caution here. It is very easy to jump to conclusions based on very little information or indeed information that is influenced by someone else's view. We need to interpret this initial data to begin to understand our own perspectives. This may tell us far more about ourselves than the place we seek to understand.

You will continue this process of initial analysis from the moment you arrive at the premises. From the outside you will absorb features of the location, buildings and grounds. As you enter you will notice the layout, decor, displays and signs. Each of these will begin to give you an idea of the philosophy, values and priorities of the place. How that institution chooses to present and manage its resources will give you insight into what it considers important. Alongside this process you will also need to analyse (reflect upon) why you have interpreted certain features in a particular way. This will again give you an insight into your own philosophy, values and priorities.

Practical task

First, think of all the features of an organisation that may influence your experience of working as part of it (both good and bad).

Now identify a real organisation, one in which you might realistically be able to undertake a placement. Explore its website and form your opinion of it.

Practical task continued

Finally, seek out a range of other information. How has this influenced your first judgement? What does this tell you about yourself?

Some features of a particular context will have a direct impact on how you will operate; some features may be more important to you than others. It may be unrealistic to try to respond to every distinctive feature, and so your next task is to prioritise. You need to ask yourself which features will offer you the best opportunity for professional development.

The number of choices you make will depend on the amount of time you have on placement, and you should be realistic in what you wish to achieve. You might wish to discuss your ambitions with an experienced colleague. Once you have identified your key issues, you need to unpack each issue in detail. You can do this by asking yourself a series of questions:

- *Why have I chosen this area as a key issue?*

- *What have I noticed about this issue in this context?*

- *Why is it important for my professional development?*

- *What concerns do I have about my own expertise in this area?*

- *What would I like to achieve by the end of the placement?*

- *How will I know whether I have been successful?*

Your answers to these questions should form a descriptive narrative which will help you to articulate your thoughts, feelings and intentions. Doing this should give you a sense of where you would like to get to during any opportunities you have for placement learning.

Continuing analysis

When you have a placement lined up and you have gone through the exercise above to understand what your personal targets are (obviously you will also have learning outcomes prescribed by your programme of study), you need to continue the process of analysis on a regular basis throughout your time in the placement context. Some people find it useful to analyse developments on a daily basis, while others prefer to do this weekly. You might wish to consider the benefits of each approach. In order to analyse your learning and the impact of the context on that learning you need to have records or data to interrogate. This goes back to the chapter where we looked at different research methods (Chapter 4). For example, you may have decided to observe how the management structure within the organisation supports your personal and professional development. The information or data that you collect could be in the form of one or several of the following:

- written notes which you jot down as you observe;

- completed structured observation schedules;

- recordings (audio and/or visual) of meetings or interviews such as appraisals;

- formal policy and procedure documents.

It is important to ensure that written notes are purely descriptive, without any attempt to interpret what you see. In the exercise below, your attention is drawn to the first stage of the process and the need for neutral description.

Practical task

(a) Compare the two sets of observation notes below.

Account 1

The students were asked to sort themselves into groups of four. There was initially some reluctance to move, suggesting a negative attitude to group working. Clearly they tended to choose to work with their friends because there was lots of laughing and chatting going on, students from ethnic minorities obviously preferring to work with each other rather than with those of different ethnicity. The body language of most students was open, suggesting they were very relaxed, whilst a few students showed very closed body language, suggesting they were uncomfortable with the situation.

Account 2

The students were asked to sort themselves into groups of four. There was a short time lag between being asked to do the task and them actually doing it, although there was lots of laughing and chatting going on. None of the groups formed comprised participants of different ethnicity. Also, only three of the eight groups were mixed-gender. Some students were sitting very quietly with their arms folded across their chests and their feet fidgeting on the floor. Others were gesticulating, laughing and sitting back in their chairs.

Consider the following:

- What features are similar in both accounts?

- What features are different?

- In what ways is account 1 more of an interpretation of events than account 2?

- What do we learn about the participants in each account?

- Which account is most useful to the practitioner? Why?

Immediately following the observation notes, we need to consider the questions it raises for us. For example, why did the students take time to form into groups? Are they not used to making such choices? Do they dislike group working? Were the instructions given clear to all?

Make a list of other questions this event might raise.

Identify possible areas of study from this exchange. For example, why do students of ethnic minorities tend to work together rather than integrating?

A reminder about ethics

We've previously discussed the need for ethical approval for research and informed consent from participants. Any work that involves collecting information about others, whether from adults or children, needs to be in line with the ethical procedures set out by the programmes you are studying (and/or the organisation within which you are working). You must ensure that the work you do meets the requirements, which are designed to ensure anonymity and protect individuals from exploitation.

Worked example

A student was on her second main placement as part of her study to become a primary teacher. A key feature of the school where she worked was that many of the children were learning English as an Additional Language (EAL). In her initial analysis she had identified three things that she planned to do to develop her skills in this area.

1. Observe a class teacher working with individual learners of EAL.

2. Read about EAL.

3. Consider the needs of the children who are learning EAL in all her lesson plans.

Using these strategies, she hoped that by the end of her placement she would achieve her target of *developing confidence in working with children who are learning EAL*.

The student devised an observation schedule that she could use when the teacher was working with the class. The schedule divided the teacher's interaction with the children into sections:

• time of observation;

• activity;

• teacher's introduction;

• group work;

• individual work;

• end of lesson.

At each stage of the lesson the student looked at how the teacher adapted her language for learners, what resources she used, how she dealt with misunderstandings, how she used other children as support and how the lesson had been modified to suit particular learners.

The student was able to take her observations and use them to draw up some principles for her own teaching and practical examples for her own lesson planning.

Reviewing professional development

Contextual analysis is cyclical in nature. That is, one set of questions will lead to investigation, which in turn may lead to further questions and investigation. During the course of any placement in a work-based context, several of these cycles may take place as you get to know the context better and discover more information. You may also find that issues that seemed important to you at the beginning of a placement become less important, and other features take on greater significance for your professional development. Do not be afraid to switch your focus in order to meet your own learning needs.

Towards the end of the placement you will want to review your progress in relation to your key issues. Of course, there will be a great deal that you have learned about professional practice, the process of learning itself and about you as a developing professional. However, it is important that you track what progress you have made in relation to those things which stood out as significant for you. You might wish to ask yourself the following series of questions:

- How has my thinking moved on in relation to my key issues?

- What do I know now that I did not before?

- How has this context developed my professional awareness and skills?

- How will it inform my future work?

- What issues will be among my next priorities?

Summary of key points

In order to learn from a work placement or any other context, it is necessary to use your critical thinking skills. Applying these skills to understanding and evaluating a context is essential for all individuals seeking to understand their professional role and boundaries.

Critical thinking skills involve careful observation and data gathering from the context, interpretation of complex environments and events, and a level of self-analysis which reveals your own values and beliefs.

References and further reading

Gambrill, E and Gibbs, L (2009) *Critical Thinking for Helping Professionals: A skills-based workbook*, 3rd edn. New York: Oxford University Press.

Jacques, K and Hyland, R (eds) (2007) *Professional Studies: Primary and early years*, 3rd edn. Exeter: Learning Matters.

Index

rhetoric 18–20
Rutz, C *et al.* 86

Salmon, G 101
scepticism 21
secondary sources 54
self-awareness 9–10, 70–1
Smith, L 77
Somekh, B 41–2
spell checkers 78–9
Spradley, J P 40
standardised tests of critical thinking skills 4, 88–9
statistical analysis 34–6
subjectivity 15–16
surveys 43–6

thematic analysis 46
third person 16–17, 59

understanding 4–5

validity of argument 8
vocabulary 60*t*

Watson-Glaser Critical Thinking Appraisal 88–9
web searching 24, 26–7
Webb, S 71, 76
websites 8
wikis 65–6, 88
writing analysis 69–79; clerical tasks 78–9; reflection 72–5; reviewing your work 69–72; structure 75–8
writing assignments 57–67; assignment briefs 59–61, 60*t*; focus 58–9, 76; learning outcomes 58, 59; mindmapping 61, 62*f*; nature of assignment 57–8; online assessments 65–6; planning 63–5; third person 16–17, 59; vocabulary 60*t*
writing structure 75; conclusion 77; introduction 76–7; main content 77–8; paragraphing 78